Date Due

	PRINTED	IN U. S. A.	

THE
NEW-ENGLAND
PRIMER
ENLARGED:

Or, an easy and pleasant
Guide to the Art of Reading.
Adorn'd with Cuts.

To which are added,
The Assembly of Divines,
and Mr. COTTON's
CATECHISM, &c.

BOSTON:

Printed by E. DRAPER, for B.
LARKIN, in *Cornhill.*

𝔗𝔥𝔢 𝔄𝔟𝔦𝔫𝔤𝔡𝔬𝔫 𝔕𝔢𝔩𝔦𝔤𝔦𝔬𝔲𝔰 𝔈𝔡𝔲𝔠𝔞𝔱𝔦𝔬𝔫 𝔗𝔢𝔵𝔱𝔰

𝔇𝔞𝔳𝔦𝔡 𝔊. 𝔇𝔬𝔴𝔫𝔢𝔶, 𝔊𝔢𝔫𝔢𝔯𝔞𝔩 𝔈𝔡𝔦𝔱𝔬𝔯

COMMUNITY TRAINING SCHOOL SERIES   NORMAN E. RICHARDSON, Editor

A History of Religious Education in Recent Times

BY

ARLO AYRES BROWN

President of the University of Chattanooga

THE ABINGDON PRESS

NEW YORK   CINCINNATI

To

MY COLLEAGUES IN RELIGIOUS EDUCATION
WHOSE EARNEST PURPOSE, SACRIFICIAL
LABOR, AND WARM FRIENDSHIP HAVE BEEN
AN UNFAILING SOURCE OF INSPIRATION

CONTENTS

The importance of education. *Jewish Education in Religion.* Teaching methods of Jesus. *Development of a System of Christian Education. Significant Early Epochs.* Early catechetical schools—The school of Alexandria —Brilliant teachers of second and third centuries— Monastic and cathedral schools—Court schools—Rise of mediæval universities. *Reformation Schools.* The Jesuit schools of the Counter Reformation—Later Reformation schools. *Summary.*

The Influence of the Reformation. Condition of education in England. *Three Types of School Policy in the Colonies. Rise and Decline of Schools in New England.* Types of schools—Textbook materials—The New England Primer—Separate schools of religion practically unknown. *Summary.*

The Rise of the Sunday-School Movement. First Sunday schools in America—Rise of Sunday-school Unions. *Movements in General Education.* Elimination of religious materials—Development of free tax-supported public-school system—Training for public-school teachers. *Sunday-School Development.* Missionary expansion—Typical Sunday schools—Methods of study— Direct Bible study—Curriculum in best schools—The Sunday-school concert. *Teacher Training.* Sunday-school aims. *Summary.*

Advance Begins with Teacher Training. A great forward step. *National Sunday School Conventions.* The

CONTENTS

8

CONTENTS

9

CONTENTS

EDITOR'S INTRODUCTION

IN preparing the material for this text the author has not been concerned chiefly with a compilation of all the available historical data of the modern religious education movement. His purpose has been rather such an interpretation of this data as would be of greatest service to the student who is interested in the functional aspect of the movement. The emphasis has been upon the significance of religious education as a challenging field of service and as marking a meaningful epoch in the historical development of the Protestant Church. The demand that the further Christianization of the present social order be brought about through the adoption of educational methods has crystallized into permanent institutions and has greatly influenced the technique of church work. The purpose of this text is to note the historical evolution of the religious education concept and to show these new forces at work. It is not *the* history, but, rather, *a* functional history of religious education in modern times.

The movement, though of comparatively recent origin in its present form, has acquired considerable practical wisdom. It has experimented with policies and leaders with the result that certain empirical values have been created. It has a history that is worthy of careful study. Any student of modern church history or any one interested in the subject of religious leadership will find this historical study illuminating and valuable.

NORMAN E. RICHARDSON.

II

AUTHOR'S INTRODUCTION

THE worker in religious education has his supreme opportunity to-day. The threatened breakdown of modern civilization because of individual and organized selfishness has led to a universal desire to develop the motive of unselfish service. Jesus of Nazareth was the most illustrious exponent of that motive ever known. Furthermore, the religion which centers about his revelation of God the Father has been the most powerful factor of the ages in helping men to develop this motive and to express it in conduct.

Men agree that if his teachings can once become universally accepted and actually applied to world problems, the world will move forward to lasting peace and prosperity. Education is the method by which men come to understand the essential facts and to establish habits of right social living. Successful Christian education universally applied would salvage what is best in our present civilization and prepare the race for achievements better than the world has yet known.

One of the principal handicaps to this end lies in the fact that so many men and women refuse to apply themselves diligently to a study of religious facts. They refuse to analyze scientifically the religious movements of the past and present, in order to ascertain the value of God-consciousness applied to the learning process.

This book is offered as a humble attempt to show what religious education has done to mold conduct within a particular region and period, what means it has used, and how these have been modified by the social movements of their day. One of the principal difficulties of a historian is to get a true perspective.

Frankly, the writer has tried to be fair and accurate but not wholly impartial. He has set definite limits for his discussion. His aim has been to stimulate action rather than simply to impart information. A wealth of interesting and significant details has been omitted. The discussion has been practically limited to describing the main stream of religious education developed for the children and youth in the Protestant churches of the United States.

It is designed for popular reading as well as for class study. A great advance in the development of religious education cannot come until many people understand the facts which have brought it to its present opportunity. No one can be more conscious of the failures of this book than the writer. But if it assists any reader to understand a great movement and to find his place in the movement, the work will not have been in vain.

Acknowledgment is gratefully made to publishers for permissions to use material from their books, to colleagues and friends who have contributed many helpful suggestions, and finally to the editors and their assistants who by their painstaking helpfulness have made this book possible.

ARLO AYRES BROWN.

University of Chattanooga, December 5, 1922.

CHAPTER I

FORERUNNERS OF MODERN RELIGIOUS EDUCATION

THE mystery of human life, how it originated and how it develops, is the most important problem with which the race deals. To the man of religious faith life comes from God. It is a sacred trust committed to the individual for his use in helping the world during a limited period. It is surrounded by ample resources, but it grows satisfactorily only when the individual masters the laws of life and uses wisely his God-given resources.

The importance of education.—Only one class of thoughtful persons can be found who willfully ignore education. This is the company of people who consider that the development of life is either an accident or that it is entirely a miracle in which intelligent human cooperation is not required. Many thoughtlessly or impatiently belittle the importance of educational processes, but the well-informed man knows that every great forward movement of history depends upon education, and that every life which comes to maturity of its powers must do so through the processes of education.

Religion has always relied upon educational methods of one sort or another to propagate itself. And the religion developed in the Old and New Testaments has been particularly dependent upon them. In no period has the interest in religious education ever been commensurate with the need, nor have the materials been well enough organized and the technique of teaching sufficiently developed. But the fact that the ancient Hebrews, together with Jesus of Nazareth and Saint Paul, relied principally upon educational methods to propagate their religious ideals is too well known to require proof.

JEWISH EDUCATION IN RELIGION

The two outstanding precedents, pointing to universal education in the fundamentals of our Christian religion, are the example of the Jewish nation and the example of Jesus of Nazareth. Where can a more stirring call to universal religious education be found than in the following verses from Deuteronomy, which constitute the "Shema" and are taught to every boy and girl in a religious Jewish home or school? "Hear, O Israel: Jehovah our God is one Jehovah: and thou shalt love Jehovah thy God with all thy heart, and with all thy soul, and with all thy might. And these words which I command thee this day, shall be upon thy heart; and thou shalt teach them diligently unto thy children, and shall talk of them when thou sitteth in thy house, and when thou walkest by the way, and when thou liest down, and when thou risest up. And thou shalt bind them for a sign upon thy hand, and they shall be for frontlets between thine eyes. And thou shalt write them upon the door posts of thy house, and upon thy gates."[1]

When Jesus of Nazareth was born this injunction had been carried out for centuries, first in the home, then in the synagogue schools, and, for more advanced students, in the rabbinical schools. The strongest circumstantial evidence indicates that Jesus himself was

[1] Deut. 6. 4–9.

carefully taught by all of these agencies.[2] In his day it was customary to have a preaching service in the synagogue on Sabbath morning and a teaching question-and-answer service on Sabbath afternoon, in addition to synagogue school sessions during the week. It was doubtless such instruction which enabled him to ask and answer questions so brilliantly in the Temple at twelve years of age.[3]

Teaching methods of Jesus.—It is not necessary to cite a particular passage to show that Jesus expected the kingdom of God on earth to be developed by teaching. His own methods were preeminently those of a teacher. His technique is an example of the most approved pedagogical methods of our own day. As an illustration compare Jesus instructing the woman of Samaria with McMurray's "four tests of a recitation."[4]

The clearest proof of his choice as to method is shown in his effort to avoid the multitude, whom he might easily have swayed by his eloquence, so that he could have more time for the instructing of twelve men.

The writer has no thought of claiming that Jesus did not resort to continuous discourse as well as to teaching by the question and answer (catechetical and discussion) method, or that he did not expect his disciples to sway multitudes with eloquent, continuous discourse. The propagation of Christianity requires both methods. Jesus used both and his immediate disciples used both. The contention of this chapter is simply that our Lord's chief reliance was placed upon the question-and-answer discussion method, supplemented by another teaching method—story-telling.

---

[2] Briggs—*History of the Study of Theology*, vol. i, pp. 17ff.
[3] Trumbull—*Yale Lectures on the Sunday School*, pp. 15ff.
[4] See McMurray—*Elementary School Standards* for these tests.

This was the approved teaching method of his day, having been used by Socrates and other Greek philosophers, and by the Jewish rabbis. It has always been the most successful teaching method, although abused and therefore seriously defective in some periods of history.

DEVELOPMENT OF A SYSTEM OF CHRISTIAN EDUCATION

This book, however, is not a history of any particular method. It is an effort to trace the development of a system of universal education in fundamental Christian truths in one country and especially within a limited period. But in order to understand the developments in modern times we must have a brief glimpse of their sources and antecedents.

Christianity makes its appeal to the whole life. Jesus expressed his goal for the individual by the phrase "abundant life." He indicated that such a life is to come by loving God completely as Father and one's neighbor as oneself. The fatherhood of God and the brotherhood of man were the ideas which he came to make clear and to establish as the guiding principles of all men. No task could be more difficult. And the student of history who accepts this interpretation of his task is obliged to form one of two conclusions, either he expected this transformation of selfish men into brothers to come instantaneously by miracle, or else he expected to use the long, slow processes of education until the human family should some day conduct their lives according to Christian standards. The process of education does not exclude great emotional crises and victories, even unexplainable transformations in human lives. Emotional development is a very vital aspect of education. At the same time men must know how to be brotherly. They must know the principles and factors which are to guide them as citizens of the kingdom of God (or democracy of God), and Jesus himself pleaded for skill in service when he warned his disciples that "the children of evil in this generation are wiser than the children of light."

SIGNIFICANT EARLY EPOCHS

When the treatment of the subject is crowded into such brief space, only the most important stages in the development of Christian education can be cited. Progress in any line of human achievement has always been uneven, sometimes by leaps and bounds and sometimes so slow that the faint-hearted have become discouraged. In tracing the history of the church as teacher the following stages are especially significant.

Early catechetical schools.—The early Christians of the apostolic period seem to have followed closely the precedents of the Jewish religionists from whom they had so recently separated. For a time Christians worshiped in Jewish synagogues, until persecution drove them out.[5] Then their Christian meetings were held in private homes, where it seems probable that the Jewish habit of conducting preaching service in the morning and a teaching service in the afternoon of their Sabbath or Sunday was followed. Women as well as men were permitted to teach, and there was, of course, no hard-and-fast distinction between the clergy and laity. Whatever distinctions there were in this early democratic church were due to the functions which the workers performed rather than to any special ordination. The disciples of Jesus were recognized as leaders, and a small number of others such as Paul, Philip, Mark,

---

[5] Hurst—*History of the Christian Church*, vol. i, pp. 142ff.

and Barnabas were added to this most influential group of leaders.[6]

Deacons were appointed to relieve the apostles from "serving tables."[7] Paul enumerates apostles, prophets, teachers, and other workers.[8] The sayings and deeds of Jesus, fundamental doctrines, prayers, hymns, Hebrew Scriptures, and letters from the apostles constituted the curriculum material.[9]

The school of Alexandria.—The most famous and most influential of the early catechetical schools was that at Alexandria of which Pantænus (about 200) was the first head, followed by Clement of Alexandria and Origen. Prior to this the Christians of Alexandria were trained in Christianity by the bishop, presbyters, and deacons through private instruction and catechetical lectures. Christians who desired a higher education had been obliged to seek it in the public rhetorical school and the university. With the coming of these brilliant, well-trained men an opportunity was given here for Christian education in rhetoric and philosophy. The widespread influence of this school is known to every student of church history.

The number of grades of catechumens in these schools has been variously estimated. Geraldine Hodgkin accepts the description given by Cardinal Newman in his *Arians of the Fourth Century*. According to Cardinal Newman, reception into full discipleship as *teleoi*, or "men in Christ," admitting to all the privileges of the church, was preceded by a period of preparation extending from two to three years. The purpose of this

---

[6] Trumbull—*Yale Lectures in the Sunday School*, p. 37.

[7] Acts 6. 1–6.

[8] 1 Cor. 12. 28.

[9] Briggs—*History of the Study of Theology*, vol. i, p. 53.

preparation was to test the obedience of the candidates and to instruct them in the principles of the revealed Christian truth. As candidates preparing for full membership, they were called catechumens because of the particular systematic way in which they were taught the fundamentals of the new faith. The instruction began with the simple principles of natural religion and advanced to the Christian mysteries.

During this introductory discipline the students passed through three grades. As *audientes* (hearers) they were given permission to hear the reading of the Scriptures and sermons in the church. Later, after receiving the imposition of hands as a sign of their progress, they were allowed to remain during the prayers and were called γουυχλινοντες (benders of the knee) or ευκομενοι (those who pray). Lastly they were taught the Lord's Prayer (the peculiar privilege of the regenerate) together with the Creed just before their baptism, and received the titles of *competentes* (the qualified), or *electi* (the chosen). But even to the last they were given only preliminary training in a formal way, for the fully developed doctrines of the Trinity, the Incarnation, and the Atonement were reserved as the exclusive privilege of the experienced Christians.[10]

A period of two (or, according to Newman, two or three) years appears to have been the ordinary time of the Christian's probation as he passed from the simple beginning to the difficult close of his course.

Brilliant teachers of second and third centuries. —Few realize how conspicuous a role the teacher played in the second century after Christ. While the apostles did not neglect instruction, they were not professional school men, but the next century brought

---

[10] Hodgkin—*Primitive Christian Education*, pp. 121ff.

to the church the services of some of the most brilliant teachers of their day. Justin, the Martyr[11] (about 114–165), is said to have been the most popular teacher in Rome. Clement of Alexandria, Origen, Tertullian, and others have left a record of educational work which is one of the brightest in church history. The church in this period was fighting for the right to live. Its teachings had to face the most searching criticism. The intellectual ones of the Roman Empire were seeking light on the meaning of life. The teachers of this day were trained in Greek philosophy and cast their Christian message into philosophic molds. The result was that the catechetical schools of Alexandria, Rome, Antioch, Nyssa, and elsewhere were crowded with students. Christianity was winning its way in the highest intellectual circles and giving the church a literature on doctrine and conduct which could be put into the minds of youth and would enable them to withstand any intellectual assaults.

It would be difficult to exaggerate the significance of this teaching epoch of the second, third, and fourth centuries. No similar emphasis upon teaching recurs until the intellectual awakening of the Renaissance and Reformation.

Monastic and cathedral schools.—While the educational passion of the early centuries subsided after Christianity had won its way to power intellectually and politically, the school movement continues but along more restricted lines. The monasteries take up the task of training bright boys for their orders and the cathedrals train boys for the work of the secular clergy. The curriculum consisted of the *Trivium*—grammar or philology, rhetoric, and logic—and the

---

[11] Briggs—*History of the Study of Theology*, vol. i, pp. 72ff.

Quadrivium—arithmetic, astronomy, geometry, and music. All of these studies, however, were taught especially for their relations to theology, music having importance in the church service, and astronomy being necessary to the calculation of Easter. Most of the schools, we are told, did not go beyond the Trivium.[12]

While civilization owes a vast debt to these monastic and cathedral schools for their contribution to learning, they did not constitute a program of education that was intended to reach all the boys and girls of the parish. They were primarily schools for the fortunate few who were to become leaders in the church.

Court schools.—Charlemagne gave impetus to the development of court schools, the celebrated Alcuin being the head of his school for a few years, withdrawing in 790. But these schools also were for the favored few who belonged to the nobility. Those who were able either sent their boys to such a school or more frequently engaged tutors to instruct them within the family castle.[13]

Rise of mediæval universities.—As an outgrowth of all three of these types of schools came the great mediæval universities. The revival of interest in both civil and canon law was greatly stimulated by the development of the universities, and was in turn greatly stimulated by them.[14] The University of Bologna became famous under Irnerius (1100–1130), a famous teacher of Roman civil law.[15]

The University of Paris grew out of the Cathedral

---

[12] Pray—*The History of Sunday Schools and of Religious Education from the Earliest Times*, pp. 73, 74.

[13] Briggs—*History of the Study of Theology*, vol. ii, pp. 11ff.

[14] For study of the mediæval universities consult Rashdall, *The Universities of Europe in the Middle Ages*, 2 vols. Macmillan Company, New York, publishers; Oxford, Clarendon Press, London.

[15] Briggs—*History of the Study of Theology*, vol. ii, p. 41.

school in Paris about the middle of the twelfth century, while Oxford developed from an obscure origin near the close of the twelfth century and Cambridge followed soon after because of a migration from Oxford. Universities at Naples, Rome, Toulouse, Padua, Lisbon, and numerous other centers were also famous. Thousands of students were in attendance at a single university, and they seem to have moved from one school to another very freely. Discipline was lax and morals low, but great leaders in church and state were trained by these institutions. The principal faculties in the schools were those of religion, law, and medicine representing the three popular professions of the day.[16]

REFORMATION SCHOOLS

The movement to give instruction in Christian fundamentals to the many instead of to the few, to the poor as well as to the rich, did not begin until the Reformation. Prior to this time no extensive learning was expected even among the rich. The favored few whose tastes were intellectual might employ tutors and secure costly manuscripts to read, but popular universal education was unknown, and not even desired.

But when the great revolt from the church came and men sought to find the seat of authority in the Bible rather than in the church, the education of individual church members became a necessity. Fortunately, the invention of printing made such universal education a possibility.

Luther, Calvin, Zwingli, Knox, and other reformers saw clearly the necessity for instructing as many of the young Christians as possible, and much attention was given to the preparation of catechetical materials

---

[16] Briggs—*History of the Study of Theology*, vol. ii, pp. 40ff.

for their training. The early period of the Reformation marks the greatest period of advance in Christian education up to that time since the second century.

The Jesuit schools of the Counter Reformation. —It must not be thought, however, that the Reformation was altogether the creator of this educational movement. The Reformation itself was in large part a result of the current intellectual ferment and passion for learning. It was first a product and then a creator of educational movements. Long before the Reformation, some of the Roman Catholic clergy had seen the necessity for more thorough instruction of the people in the Christian fundamentals.

But when the Reformation came the church was forced to combat learning with learning. Ignatius Loyola saw the opportunity of winning back the lost multitudes through teaching their boys and girls. The supreme tools of the Jesuits were their schools, and following their leadership, the Roman Catholic Church won back through superior school-teaching great multitudes and whole nations that seemed to be lost to her forever.

Carlo Borromeo (1538–1584), Archbishop of Milan, was a very enthusiastic educational reformer and held a Sunday school in the cathedral of Milan Sunday afternoons with hundreds of pupils of both sexes divided into small classes under the instruction of a clergyman and one or more lay assistants. He promoted these schools throughout his diocese.

Later Reformation schools.—But the pendulum of interest swung away from education again. The catechisms, which were meant to be only skeletons to guide the discussions of teachers, became the whole body of curriculum material. The leaders became indifferent to teaching, perhaps because the opportunity of settling disputes by preaching about them was too fascinating for these leaders to withstand. At any rate the churches of the Reformation lost much of their zeal for teaching the young, with the result that in the seventeenth and eighteenth centuries they reaped a harvest of religious indifference and moral degeneracy which seems incredible, following so soon after a great spiritual awakening.

Near the close of the seventeenth century and early in the eighteenth we find a revival of vital religious experience and interest in religious education in the movement of Pietism in Germany led by Spener, the Moravian revival led by Count Zinzendorf, and the Wesleyan movement in England. The Moravian Brethren gave especial attention to the instruction of the young, dividing the converts into groups of five. John Wesley, acknowledging his debt to the Moravians, adopted a plan of class meetings for his societies. When the Sunday-school movement was being started by Robert Raikes he was one of the first to see its possibilities and joined vigorously in its promotion.

SUMMARY

We have seen in this chapter that the example of the ancient Hebrews and of Jesus points to education as the outstanding method for developing religious character. We have noted how the apostles made the church of their period a teaching church and how the next few generations succeeding them produced brilliant teachers of Christianity. We have also followed briefly the educational movement inspired and to a large degree directed by the church, through monastic, cathedral, and court schools and through great universities. We have noted the intellectual ferment which produced the Reformation and the great movements for the training of multitudes both in the Reformation churches and also in the Roman Catholic Church. Lastly, we have noted a decline in educational interest in the later Reformational period and the promise of a revival of interest. This brings us to the colonial period in America.

Every reader has probably been impressed with the fact that from the Jewish schools before Christ down through the Reformation period practically all of the schools have had religious education as one of their dominant aims and have been under the direction of church leaders. There has been in the period which we have discussed no general education separate from religious education.

Questions for discussion:

1. To what extent has the perpetuity of the Jewish race been due to its emphasis upon education in religion?
2. What evidence is there to show that Jesus depended primarily upon teaching methods to win the world?
3. Discuss the technique of Jesus as a teacher.
4. To what extent did Saint Paul depend upon teaching methods to win and develop followers of Jesus?
5. How do you account for the strong appeal which Christianity made to the intellectual classes in the second and third centuries A.D.?
6. Discuss the significance to the cause of religious education of the various types of schools described in this chapter.

7. Trace any tendencies to separation of religion from general education which you may be able to discover in the epochs cited.
8. How do you account for the close identification of religion with general education through the centuries that have been mentioned?

Brief bibliography of selected references:

Briggs—*History of the Study of Theology*, Vols. I, II. Charles Scribner's Sons, New York, 1916.

Cope—*The Evolution of the Sunday School*. The Pilgrim Press, Boston, 1911.

Trumbull—*Yale Lectures on the Sunday School*. Charles Scribner's Sons, New York, 1904. (Copyright, 1888.)

Hurst—*History of the Christian Church*, Vol. I. Eaton and Mains, New York, 1901.

Hodgkin—*Primitive Christian Education*. T. & T. Clark, Edinburgh, 1906.

Pray—*The History of Sunday Schools and of Religious Education from the Earliest Times*. William Crosby and H. P. Nichols, Boston, 1847.

Rashdall—*The Universities of Europe in the Middle Ages*, Vols. I, II. The Macmillan Company, New York; Oxford, Clarendon Press, London, 1895.

Meyer—*The Graded Sunday School in Principle and Practice*. The Methodist Book Concern, New York.

CHAPTER II

EARLY RELIGIOUS EDUCATION IN AMERICA

THE story of religious education in the American colonies is the story of the development of general education as well. The two movements were inseparably united for the simple reason that the colonists had never known of their being otherwise.

THE INFLUENCE OF THE REFORMATION

The modern educational development received its greatest impulse from the Protestant Reformation. When the seat of authority in religion was transferred from an "infallible church" to an "infallible book" the necessity for universal education became at once manifest. It might require centuries before the great nations should develop an adequate program of education for all the people, but the nations which accepted the Protestant interpretation of religion were of necessity committed to such a policy.

The reason why progress was slow lay in the fact that the world was not yet committed to the principles of a democratic society. The people could believe in universal salvation for slave, pauper, and noble, but that salvation would lie in the "hereafter"; it could not apply to everyday life. Not only in England but throughout Europe many in the seventeenth and eighteenth centuries would have agreed with Mandeville, in his "Essay on Charity Schools," that "there is no Need for any Learning at all for the meanest Ranks of Mankind: Their Business is to Labor, not to Think. Their Duty is to do what they are commanded, to fill up the most servile Posts, and to perform the lowest Offices and Drudgeries of Life for the Conveniency of their Superiors; and Common Nature gives them knowledge enough for this Purpose."[1]

We find immediately following the Reformation a slow but steady movement toward universal free education—slow because it was so inimical to the desires of the privileged classes, but steady because of the religious passion of the Protestants that all be taught to read the Scriptures. As the worth of the individual came to be more generally recognized and as the nations developed more democratic forms of government, the movement became greatly accelerated, because the necessities of a democratic state also demanded an educated people.

Condition of education in England.—Since by far the majority of the colonists came from England, we would expect to find the essential features of the English system of education reproduced in America. This is exactly the case. Hence we should give brief consideration to the educational program of England at this time. Free education in England at the beginning of the seventeenth century was practically unknown and considered undesirable. The rich and the fortunate were tutored in private homes, then sent to a Latin-grammar school to be prepared for Oxford or Cambridge. Education for the poorer classes was opposed because the poor were expected to do only menial labor for the more fortunate, and it was feared that education would unfit them for menial service.

However, the poor were expected to receive education

---

[1] Quoted from Graves—*A History of Education in Modern Times*, p. 40. Copyright by The Macmillan Company. Used by permission.

for their labor through the apprentice system, and in time "pauper" or "charity" schools were started as a matter of self-protection or as the result of some patron's generous impulse. The state was expected to assume no responsibility for education and the church assumed none for the education of the rich. These were able to take care of themselves through the means indicated. But the church did come to see that to some extent it was responsible for educating the poor. In 1698 a "Society for the Promotion of Christian Knowledge" was founded, assuming as its chief project "to set up catechetical schools for the education of poor children." The teachers of these schools were required to be members of the Church of England, and to be approved by the minister of the parish in which each lived. Each master was required to teach the catechism in addition to the regular work in reading, writing, and "the Grounds of Arithmetic to fit them for Service as Apprentices." "Parents were also required under penalty of their children being dismissed from the school, to see that the children did not absent themselves save for sickness, and that they came to school cleanly and neat. Besides being educated the pupils were clothed, boarded, and at times even lodged."[2] Such were the beginnings of free education in England, and these types of education both for the poor and also for the rich became the standard in many of the colonies, however with modifications that will be noted.

THREE TYPES OF SCHOOL POLICY IN THE COLONIES

The beginnings of education in the American colonies follow, in the main, three general types. In Virginia,

---

[2] Graves—*A History of Education in Modern Times*, p. 38.

Maryland, and generally in the Southern States the English policy approved by the upper classes held sway. This policy was that the poor should not be given education except as apprentices and that the rich should provide it for themselves through private tutors, and through grammar schools and colleges without interference by the church or state. The State of Virginia, at the beginning, concerned herself principally with the establishment of the College of William and Mary. Although there were praiseworthy efforts as far back as 1616 for the education of the children, they produced little, for as late as 1671 Governor Berkeley, when questioned concerning instruction in the colony, said: "The same course that is taken in England out of towns; every man according to his ability instructing his children. . . . But I thank God there are no free schools nor printing, and I hope we shall not have these hundred years; for learning has brought disobedience and heresy and sects into the world, and printing has divulged them and libels against the best government. God keep us from both!"[3]

The second type was that of the parochial school which held sway in the middle colonies of Pennsylvania, Delaware, New Jersey, New York, and among the Roman Catholics of Maryland. Here the population was much less homogeneous than in either the Southern or Northern colonies. The Germans of many sects early settled in Pennsylvania beside the English, and the Dutch were the first settlers of New York. Roman Catholics predominated in Maryland and were strong in Pennsylvania, while New Jersey and Delaware were

---

[3] Dexter—*History of Education in the United States*, p. 10. Copyright by ·The Macmillan Company, publishers. Used by permission.

settled by a variety of nationalities and sects such as Swedes, Finns, Dutch Quakers, Anglicans, and Scotch Presbyterians.

The communities being so heterogeneous, a common school for the community dominated by one sect was out of the question. The sects and nationalities were interested in education, but the parochial system was the only one that they knew or that seemed possible to them. That religion should receive marked attention in this type of school as it did, is exactly what we would expect.

The third type was the common-school type of New England which formed the basis of our present public school system. Here the communities were in the early days homogeneous and intensely religious. The community was a small state under religious control. Hence a parochial school and community school would be identical. Dexter calls attention to the fact that "never since, in the history of our country, has the population as a class been so highly educated as during the first half-century of the Massachusetts settlements. One man in every two hundred and fifty had been graduated from an English university, and both clergy and laity had brought from home enviable reputations for superior service both in church and college."[4]

As early as 1635 the Massachusetts Bay Colony in a town meeting voted "therefore brother Philemon[5] Parmount shall be interested to become schoolmaster for the nurturing of children with us." In 1836 Harvard College was started for the preparation of

---

[4] Dexter—*History of Education in the United States*, p. 24.

[5] *Ibid.*, p. 25.

ministers, and in 1842 a very significant law was enacted, a portion of which was as follows:

This court taking into consideration the great neglect of many parents and masters in training up their children in learning and labor, and other employments which may be profitable to the commonwealth, do hereupon order and decree that in every town the chosen men appointed for managing the prudential affairs of the same shall henceforth stand charged with the care of the redress of this evil, so as they shall be sufficiently punished by fines for the neglect thereof upon presentment of the grand jury, or any other information or complaint in any court within this jurisdiction; and for this end they, or the greater number of them, shall have the power to take account from time to time of all parents and masters, and of their children concerning their calling and employment of their children, especially of their ability to read and understand the principles of religion and the capital laws of this country, and to impose fines upon such as shall refuse to render such accounts to them when they shall be required; and they shall have power, with consent of any court or the magistrate, to put forth apprentices the children of such as they shall (find) not to be able and fit to employ and bring them up . . ."[6]

Of still greater significance is the Massachusetts School Ordinance of 1647:

It being one of the chief projects of that old deluder Satan to keep men from the knowledge of the Scriptures, as in former times by keeping them in an unknown tongue, so in these later times by persuading from the use of tongues, that so at least the true sense and meaning of the original might be clouded by false gloss is of saint-seeming deceivers, that learning may not be buried

---

[6] Dexter—*History of Education in the United States*, p. 584, Appendix B.

in the grave of our fathers in the church and commonwealth, the Lord assisting our endeavors:

It is therefore ordered, That every township in this jurisdiction, after the Lord hath increased them to the number of fifty householders, shall then forthwith appoint one within their town to teach all such children as shall resort to him to write and read, whose wages shall be paid either by the parents or masters of such children, or by the inhabitants in general, by way of supply, as the major part of those that order the prudentials of the town shall appoint: *Provided,* Those that send their children be not oppressed by paying much more than they can have them taught for in other towns; and *It is further ordered,* That where any town shall increase to the number of one hundred families or householders, they shall set up a grammar school, the master thereof being able to instruct youth, so far as they may be fitted, for the university: *Provided,* That if any town neglect the performance here of above one year, that every such town shall pay five pounds to the next school until they shall perform this order.[7]

RISE AND DECLINE OF SCHOOLS IN NEW ENGLAND

The other New England States, with the exception of Rhode Island, followed, in the main, the pattern set by Massachusetts. The Connecticut School Law of 1650 was modeled very closely after the Massachusetts law of 1647. However, the eighteenth century witnessed a decline in the zeal and achievements of Massachusetts for several reasons. In the first place, the hard conditions of life in this new country steadily wore down some of the interest in education and general culture, while the immigration of new sects broke up the homogeneity of the community groups.

---

[7] *Ibid.,* p. 585.

A further factor in the decline was the development of the district-school system. As the communities grew the population became more scattered, and people demanded that the schools be made more convenient for them. At first this demand was met by moving the schools from one district to another for short periods, and gradually it led to the establishment of district schools authorized by law. It is easy to see how the district system would create very uneven school opportunities. In thickly populated districts the school of the "three R's" and the higher Latin-grammar school were possible, but in sparsely settled districts only the very elementary school was apt to be developed. Writers of educational history generally admit that the district system proved to be a distinct handicap to Massachusetts, and permitted New York to pass her in educational efficiency at the close of the colonial period.

Types of schools.—Near the close of the colonial period the following types of schools were common to all parts of the country, although with very different degrees of efficiency: the "Dame School," conducted by some woman in a private home, where the youngest children were taught their letters and the simplest elements of reading and writing; the "School of the Three R's," or common school, where reading, writing, and arithmetic were the principal subjects; the Latin-grammar school, believed by many to be the most efficient part of the school system in this period. In this school Latin was given especial prominence, but other cultural subjects selected to prepare one for college were taught. These schools became the basis of the most typical American educational institution, the American high school, and for a long period furnished the teachers for the elementary schools. Above these stood the college, founded first especially to prepare men for the ministry. But the curriculum was soon broadened to prepare for the other learned professions of law and medicine and for the life of a "cultured gentleman."

Textbook materials.—The curriculum materials for this period were predominantly religious. The earliest book used was not a book at all but a paddle-shaped piece of wood covered with a printed leaf of paper protected by a thin sheet of transparent horn. Because of the covering it was known as the *Hornbook* and contained principally the alphabet and the Lord's Prayer. After learning to read from this the pupil passed to the catechism and the Bible. These, according to Cubberley, "constituted the entire range of reading in the schools."[8]

The New England Primer.—Next to the Bible the most influential book in New England during the colonial period was *The New England Primer*, which soon superseded the *Hornbook*, and was used very generally by schools in all of the colonies except those under control of the Church of England.

In the "Foreword" of a *New England Primer*, "Twentieth Century Reprint," by Ginn & Company, we read this apt characterization of the book and its influence: "*The New England Primer* was one of the greatest books ever published. It went through innumerable editions; it reflected in a marvelous way the spirit of the age that produced it, and contributed perhaps more than any other book except the Bible

---

[8] Cubberley—*Public Education in the United States*, p. 30. Houghton Mifflin Company, publishers; used by permission.

to the molding of those sturdy generations that gave to America its liberty and its institutions."[9]

The *New England Primer* contains the alphabet, easy syllables, words of one to five syllables, the Lord's Prayer, and Apostles' Creed, words and couplets illustrated by crude but very interesting wood cuts, a picture and story of the martyrdom of John Rogers, prayers for children including grace before and after meals, William Cotton's *Catechism*, and many poems or sentences calculated to impress religious truth upon the minds of the young. Much attention is given to preparing for death, as the following indicates:

> "I in the burying place may see
> Graves shorter there than I.
> From death's arrest no age is free;
> Young children too may die.
> My God, may such an awful sight
> Awakening be to me!
> Oh! that by early grace I might
> For death preparèd be."[10]

But there are also many admonitions calculated to guide the child in this life. For example the following:

Three Choice Sentences

1. Praying will make us leave Sinning or Sinning will make us leave Praying.

2. Our Weaknesses and Inabilities break not the Bond of our Duties.

3. What we are afraid to speak before men we should be afraid to speak before God.[11]

---

[9] *The New England Primer*, Twentieth Century Reprint, published by Ginn & Company. Used by permission of Le Roy Phillips, publisher, Boston, the present owner of copyright.

[10] Used by permission of Le Roy Phillips, publisher.

[11] *Ibid.*

The prayer which so many readers have learned in childhood, "Now I lay me down to sleep," is in this book, and also Watts' Cradle Hymn, "Hush, my dear, lie still and slumber."

Wherever the *New England Primer* was used there was no need for supplementary Sunday schools of religious instruction, for the *Primer* was essentially a child's book of religion. Some of it was not within the reach of the child's understanding, and the religious teacher of to-day would find it too somber, dealing too much with death and too little with life here under the heavenly Father's guidance. But clearly it must have put "the fear of God" into young hearts, and prepared them for heroic Christian living.

While the *New England Primer* and the Bible maintained their supremacy through the colonial period, after 1750 there was a marked decline of interest in the religious materials due in large part to the introduction of a new type of text book, Dillworth's *A New Guide to the English Tongue.*

Separate schools of religion practically unknown. —A church-school system apart from the regular day-school system was practically unknown in this period. We read of churches in New England which held a preaching service on Sunday morning and a teaching service Sunday afternoon, somewhat similar to the custom of the Jews in the time of Christ. But no effort was made to develop religious schools apart from the day schools of the colony. The reason for this is too apparent to require discussion.

SUMMARY

In attempting to summarize the values of the colonial period in the development of religious education, one must recognize the following items as vital factors in this department:

First, the educational methods and types of schools were an inheritance from the Old World, especially from the mother country, England.

Second. Local conditions made the development of schools very irregular in the various colonies with outstanding differences between the southern, the middle, and the northern colonies. In the South pauper schools developed slowly while academies and colleges, especially in Virginia and Maryland, made a fair gain, but free common school education had little development. In the Middle colonies, parochial schools usually for poor children were numerous, but common schools for all of the people came slowly. In the North, New England, the common school developed early and became the type of America's public-school system. However, this development was seriously retarded near the close of the period because of hard conditions of living, the new elements in the population, and the unfortunate district system of school control.

Third. The aim of education in all of the colonies seems to have been primarily religious, the biblical material constituting a large part of the curriculum. As in the Old World, those who were principally interested in education for the young were those possessing the deepest religious interest. It will always be a debatable question whether their chief interest was to prepare the child for death or for life on this earth, but in either event the materials used were the same.

Fourth. No significant development of religious instruction on Sunday is noted for this period because the week-day school work was primarily religious. Some Sunday afternoon teaching services are known to have been conducted, but they did not seem to be needed, and there was no significant development along this line until the next period.

Fifth. The almost complete uniting of church and state in school matters is of striking importance because we will trace in the following chapters a development which led to complete separation of church schools and religious education from the schools of the state. In this chapter we have noted how the pendulum swung to one extreme. In the next chapter we will note how it gradually swung to the other extreme, where it has remained until the present.

Questions for discussion:

1. How do you account for the length of time required before universal education became a common aim among Christians?
2. Discuss the influence of the Protestant Reformation upon the development of a system of education for the poor as well as for the rich.
3. What other factors stimulated the development of a passion for universal education?
4. Describe educational conditions in England in the seventeenth century.
5. Investigate further the early school system of the Southern, the Middle, and the New England colonies. In which of these systems was religion most effectively taught?
6. What is your estimate of the *New England Primer* as a text work for the young in the colonial period?
7. Why was there a tendency to break away from the exclusive use of religious materials near the close of this period?

8. What types of character would you expect the school systems of this period to produce?
9. What permanent effects of the religious element in the colonial-school system can you see in the public-school system of to-day?

Brief bibliography of selected reference:

Cubberley—*Public Education in the United States*. Houghton Mifflin Company, Boston, 1919.

Graves—*A History of Education in Modern Times*. The Macmillan Company, New York, 1919. (Copyright, 1913.)

Dexter—*History of Education in the United States*. The Macmillan Company, New York, 1919. (Copyright, 1904.)

Brown—*The Making of Our Middle Schools*. Longmans, Green and Co., New York, 1918. (Copyright, 1902.)

Monroe—*Text-Book in the History of Education*. The Macmillan Company, New York, 1916. (Copyright, 1905.)

The New England Primer, Twentieth Century Reprint. Ginn & Company. Le Roy Phillips, publisher.

Ford—*The New England Primer*, Dodd, Mead & Co., New York, 1899.

CHAPTER III

RELIGIOUS EDUCATION FROM 1784-1860

THE following comment of a writer who is speaking of a Sunday school as he knew it in 1817 will lead us into the heart of our problem as we attempt to discover how effectively religious education was being administered in the early days of the nineteenth century.

SUNDAY-SCHOOL PROGRESS

The thoughtful inquirer after possible improvements in the Sunday school cannot but be struck with the fact that very few new features have been added to it for the past fifty years. A first-class Sunday school of to-day differs very little in its essential features from a first-class school of half a century ago. This statement may strike some ears strangely, but it is nevertheless historically true. The institution is only about fourscore years of age. Like many other majestic things, it began obscurely. It was simply a device to keep a few juvenile Sabbath idlers from the street and to teach them the elements of secular and religious knowledge—a sort of Sabbath substitute for the absence of week-day schools for the poor. Mr. Wesley, with other good men of those times, soon perceived its capabilities for higher purposes. He attached it to his societies, abolished its more secular features, substituted voluntary for hired teachers, and made it substantially what it is to-day. Though not an old man, the writer's recollection embraces a period of nearly fifty years—say forty-eight. He was so long ago a scholar in a school which possessed nearly everything we have in our best schools to-day.

1. It was governed by a Sunday-school society composed of its officers and teachers, with the pastor as president *ex officio*.

2. It had monthly teachers' meetings for business, and teachers' prayer meetings for devotional purposes. It also had its public anniversaries, in which the children sang and took other parts in the exercises.

3. The school was organized into classes, and had its superintendent, secretary, and librarians—with this improvement over modern schools: each class had two instructors, namely, a teacher and an assistant teacher, the latter quite a youth, generally, and a candidate for the office of teacher.

4. It had its Bible class under the name of "Monitors' Class," composed of the senior scholars, from among whom assistant teachers were selected.

5. The school had a series of catechetical textbooks, beginning with the "Milk for Babes," and ending with an advanced work on Christian doctrines, the scholars graduating from class to class as rapidly as they mastered the textbooks.

6. The school had a library of several hundred volumes. It also had its periodicals and reward books.

7. Singing was made a specialty in it.

8. The children were all taken to church in the morning and had a religious service, with an appropriate address after the hour for instruction in the afternoon.

9. The school met in large upstair rooms, fitted up and kept exclusively for its use.

Such was a first-class Sunday school nearly fifty years ago. What has been added to first-class Sunday schools since?

(1) The infant department. (2) The Sunday-school paper instead of or in addition to the Magazine. (3) The question-book, requiring the children to use the Bible as the textbook proper. (4) Adult Bible classes.

These four features are all that modern times have given to the institution, unless we add training classes or institutes for the instruction of teachers, which, being only partially and exceptionally employed either in England or America, can hardly as yet be regarded as really belonging to the institution.

Thus it appears that so far as the addition of new features is concerned, little progress has been made in fifty years. We venture to remark that, in all probability, the next fifty years will scarcely be more productive of novelties than the last. The institution, like the church itself, is molded into the form which, however it may be modified in detail, will be retained to the end of time. It is, most likely, incapable of being essentially altered without being perverted from its true relation to Christianity.

Wherein, then, has the institution made progress if not in its essential features? We will answer this question in our next number.[1]

No one imagines that so good a school as is herein described was typical of the period, but it is significant that such a Sunday school existed at all, and there is abundant evidence that other schools were just as well developed as this one.

THE RISE OF THE SUNDAY-SCHOOL MOVEMENT

To understand how this development came about let us review briefly the religious developments in England in the last quarter of the eighteenth century. Historians unanimously paint a black picture of moral conditions in England during the latter part of the eighteenth century. Illiteracy, irreligion, and degeneracy seem to have joined hands in this period. The Wesleyan Revival started a strong counter current, which, according

[1] *Sunday School Journal*, November, 1865, vol. i, p. 13.

to the historian Green, saved England from the horrors of another French Revolution.

However, the Wesleyan Revival was only one of the movements which eventually turned back the tide of infidelity, formalism, and vicious living. One of the most significant factors was the movement by Robert Raikes. Being distressed over the ignorance and bestiality of poor children who had no chance to learn better habits, in 1780 he gathered some of them off the streets into his own home for study on Sunday. He hired four teachers to do the instructing and kept the children at their tasks from 10 to 12 A.M., and from 1 to 4 P.M. After three years of experimenting he was so enthusiastic over the results that he made known his plan through the *Gloucester Journal,* of which he was the editor and publisher.

He was not the first to conduct a school on Sunday and use religious materials for the curriculum. As we have seen in a previous chapter, the Jews and the early Christians did the same. Borromeo and others held Sunday schools with conspicuous success. Some isolated efforts in this direction had also been put forth in England, Wales, and America before Robert Raikes ever tried his plan. But his newspaper gave publicity to the school and the time was ripe to propagate the movement.

The poor of England were in an unbelievable state of ignorance and degradation with practically no opportunity to learn except through the apprentice system. There were no free schools except very rarely where some generous individual could not be satisfied without attempting to relieve their needs. Robert Raikes began his work after a good woman called his attention to the savagery of the children in her neighborhood.

46

In writing to Colonel Townley on November 25, 1783, Robert Raikes stated that they had no rules except to require the children to come to the school on Sunday "as clean as possible." Clean hands, clean face, and the hair combed were expected. "If you have no clean shirt, come in what you have on." A clean shirt was desirable but not obligatory.[2] He believed that habits of orderliness and good conduct were essential to permanent reformation of character.

Many protested vehemently against giving such instruction to the poor and against profaning the Lord's Day by such secular work. Some of the church leaders put up the bitterest opposition. But a vast number of people hailed the school as the harbinger of a new day. And later historians have not hesitated to call it the beginning of the free public-school movement of England.

Within a year after Robert Raikes announced his plan in *The Gentleman's Magazine*, 1784, a society for the propagation of the plan had been organized, taking as its name "The Sunday-School Society of London." Some of the objects of the schools promoted by this society were the prevention of vice, the encouragement of industry and virtue, the bringing of men "cheerfully to submit to their stations," obeying the laws of God and their country, the leading of pupils in "the pleasant paths of religion here," and the preparing of them "for a glorious eternity."

But the greatest obstacles to the prosperity of Sunday schools at the beginning were the difficulties of obtaining suitable teachers and the expense of hiring them. They were paid at the rate of one shilling and sixpence or two shillings each Sunday, and from 1786 to

---

[2] Harris—*Robert Raikes: The Man and His Work*, pp. 309, 310.

1800 the Sunday-School Society alone paid upward of seventeen thousand dollars for hired teachers. But John Wesley and others who saw in this a powerful instrument for instruction in religion substituted volunteer for paid teachers, and with this obstacle removed the movement spread with remarkable success. In 1787 the number known to be connected with these schools was about two hundred and fifty thousand.

First Sunday schools in America.—While several schools or classes of religious instruction meeting on Sunday are known to have existed previously, the first Sunday school patterned after the Robert Raikes plan[3] so far as the writer can learn, was the school established by William Elliot in 1785 in his own home, where each Sabbath afternoon he instructed the white boys "bound-out" to him, and the girls in his charge, together with his own children. Soon the children of neighbors and friends were admitted. The Negro slaves and servants were similarly taught at another hour. All were taught the rudiments of reading in order that they might be able to read God's Word for themselves, the Bible being practically the only textbook in the school. This school in 1801 was transferred to Burton-Oak Grove Methodist Church, Bradford's Neck, Accomac County, Virginia, Mr. Elliot coming with it as its first superintendent in the new church. According to Miss Wardle, the year 1916 recorded one hundred and thirty-two years of aggressive Sunday-school effort for this one community[4].

---

[3] Marianna C. Brown, in *Sunday-School Movements in America* (pp. 19, 21), lists the following places in America as having Sunday schools before the Robert Raikes plan was introduced: Plymouth, Massachusetts, 1695; Roxbury, Massachusetts, 1674; Ephrata, Lancaster County, Pennsylvania, 1740. The latter established by Ludwig Thacker.

[4] Wardle—*History of the Sunday School Movement in the Methodist Episcopal Church*, p. 46.

The second Sunday school was established by Francis Asbury in 1786 in the home of Thomas Crenshaw, Hanover County, Virginia, a school of religion for slaves. In 1790 the Methodist Conference in Charleston, South Carolina, gave official recognition to such schools by the following action in question and answer form "What can be done in order to instruct poor children (whites and blacks) to read? Let us labor, as the heart and soul of one man, to establish Sunday schools, in or near the place of public worship. Let persons be appointed by the bishops, elders, deacons, or preachers to teach (*gratis*) all that will attend and have capacity to learn, from six o'clock in the morning till ten; and from two o'clock in the afternoon till six, where it does not interfere with public worship.

"The council shall compile a proper schoolbook to teach them learning and piety."[5]

Pray cites the following early Sunday-school enterprises: December 26, 1790, The First Day or Sunday-School Society organized in Philadelphia. Officers were elected on January 11, 1791, Bishop White as president. In March, 1791, the first school opened. In 1793 the society voted "that the instructions to be given in these schools should be confined to reading and writing from the Bible; but for such scholars as had not learned to read, spelling books and primers might be used."[6]

In 1797 a Sunday school was organized at Pawtucket, Rhode Island; in 1803, one at Hudson, New York; in 1810, one at Beverly, Massachusetts; in 1812 the first one in Boston, West Parish; in 1812, at Brunswick,

---

[5] Minutes of the Methodist Conferences annually held in America, 1773 to 1794, inclusive, published 1795, p. 147.

[6] Pray—*History of Sunday Schools and of Religious Education from the Earliest Times*, pp. 206ff.

Maine; in 1813, at Albany; in 1814, at New York and Wilmington.

Rise of Sunday-School Unions.—Little educational progress is to be reported for America between the War for American Independence and the War of 1812. Political conditions were so unstable and the financial burdens upon the people so staggering that education was comparatively a neglected interest. Nevertheless, there was a growing interest in Sunday-school education, as we have noted, due doubtless to response to a desperate need, but the movements under way were halted by the new war. However, when this war had been won the nation faced the future with a new confidence and began to take up vigorously the development of education along with other vital interests. Religious education shared this rebirth of interest, and we find "Unions" for the promotion of Sunday-school work being organized in leading cities such as New York, 1816; Boston, 1816; Philadelphia, 1817. In 1824 the American Sunday-School Union, which was destined to play so large a part in the nation-wide promotion of the movement, was organized. It was an outgrowth of the Sunday and Adult School Union, which was organized in Philadelphia in 1817. By the year 1830 some of the leading denominations had also organized Sunday-School Unions and the Sunday school was in the midst of an era of rapidly growing popularity.

MOVEMENTS IN GENERAL EDUCATION

Before tracing further the development of the Sunday school, let us study the progress of general education. We have already noted near the close of the colonial period a marked tendency on the part of the common schools to get away from religious instruction. The

introduction of new textbooks displacing the Bible and
the *primer* was one of the greatest factors. Dillworth's
A New Guide to the English Tongue, published in England in 1740, and introduced into the colonies in 1750,
was the first of these textbooks to displace the Bible.
It contained words for spelling and a number of fables.
In 1783 the first distinctively American textbook of this
kind appeared, Noah Webster's *American Spelling Book*,
which met with very great popularity.

Other textbooks followed, such as Webster's *The
Little Reader's Assistant* (1790), *The Columbian Primer*
(1802), *The Franklin Primer* (1802), Bingham's *American
Preceptor* (1794), and *The Columbian Orator* (1806).
Cubberley says of these: "*The Preceptor* was a graded
reader and soon replaced the Bible as an advanced reading book, while *The Orator* was one of the earliest of
a long list of books containing selections from poetry
and prose for reading and declamation. These books
suited well the new democratic spirit of the times, and
became very popular."[7] Textbooks in arithmetic, grammar, and geography also appeared about the same time,
and a little later books on United States history.

Elimination of religious materials.—So completely
does the Bible seem to have been displaced in the
common schools by the beginning of the nineteenth
century that the Rev. Thomas Thatcher of Dedham,
Massachusetts, in an ordination sermon for the Rev.
Joseph Tuckerman protests that "the reading of Scripture in schools is either wholly neglected or reduced to
an inferior and disgusting part of puerile duty."[8]

The story of the divorcement of general education

---

[7] Cubberley—*Public Education in the United States*, p. 218.   Houghton Mifflin
Company, publishers.   Used by permission.

[8] Pray—*History of Sunday Schools and of Religious Education*, p. 198.

from religious education and the development of an American public-school system independent of any church control with Bible study eliminated is one of the most significant chapters in educational history. That a public-school system independent of any sectarian control was necessary seems to the writer to be self-evident. That the elimination of direct instruction in the Bible and all other religious materials was necessary is not so evident. The reasons for such elimination are apparent, but the necessity cannot be proved, and the result has been a very serious defect in a great and highly effective public-school system. It seems to be the story of a reaction which went too far.

Early education in America was too completely under church control. It was also too aristocratic. The secondary schools and colleges had little interest beyond that of preparing students for the "learned professions or for the occupation of a gentleman." That the rising tide of democratic ideals in this new land would overthrow such a conception of education was inevitable. Furthermore, the churches of this era have themselves to blame in large part for being so intolerant that they could not agree upon the common religious fundamentals which might be taught in a public-school system.

The rising tide of democratic feeling, the extension of universal suffrage, the rapid growth of cities, and the increasing demands of rapidly developing industrial interests were also very important factors in determining the new forms of public education.

Development of free, tax-supported public-school system.—The most significant stages in the struggle for free, tax-supported, nonsectarian, state-controlled schools, according to Cubberley, are as follows:

"(1) The battle for tax support. (2) The battle to

eliminate the pauper-school idea. (3) The battle to make the schools entirely free. (4) The battle to establish State supervision. (5) The battle to eliminate sectarianism. (6) The battle to extend the system upward. (7) Addition of the State university to crown the system."[9]

In describing this development Cubberley says: "In 1825 such schools were the distant hope of statesmen and reformers; in 1850 they were becoming an actuality in almost every Northern State. The twenty-five years intervening marked a period of public agitation and educational propaganda, of many hard legislative fights, of a struggle to secure desired legislation and then to hold what had been secured, of many bitter contests with church and private school interests, which felt that their 'vested rights' were being taken away from them, and of occasional referenda in which the people were asked, at the next election, to advise the Legislature what to do. Excepting the battle for the abolition of slavery, perhaps no question has ever been before the American people for settlement which caused so many antagonisms."[10] The battle was clearly won in the North by the middle of the century, but the Civil War so held up the development of the system that it was not until the close of the war that the public-school system of America began its era of progress.

One of the significant experiments of this period in the field of general education was the inauguration of what is known as the Lancaster System. Prior to this time most of the instruction given in the schools had been by the method of individual recitations. Joseph

---

[9] Cubberley—*Public Education in the United States*, p. 128.

[10] *Ibid.*, p. 119.

Lancaster and another Englishman, Dr. Anderson Bell, at about the same time perceived the advantage of using monitors. Since drills were the main feature of instruction, all that was necessary was to arrange the materials in suitable form for drills, and to prepare as drill-masters some of the brightest pupils. Originally the plan was to teach only reading and the catechism, but it was soon extended to teach writing, simple sums, spelling, and higher subjects. So enthusiastic were the supporters of this plan that many expected this system to create a new era in education.

But the net result of the movement was far less than many anticipated. It was very popular from 1810 to 1830, but had lost much of its popularity by 1840. However, it did leave certain lasting benefits. It emancipated the common schools from the slow method of one pupil reciting a whole lesson privately to his teacher. By enabling one teacher to guide more pupils it helped to make practical the idea of a free-school system. Furthermore, the agitation in favor of the system had a wholesome effect in interesting the public, and lastly it proved to be a forerunner of a teacher-training system.

Training for public-school teachers.—No movement in general education was more influential in improving both public schools and in the long run Sunday schools than the teacher-training movement as developed through State normal schools. The first teacher-training school was a private institution established in 1823 by the Rev. Samuel R. Hall in Concord, Vermont. This he maintained at Concord until 1830, when he moved the school to Andover, Massachusetts, until 1837, and finally to Plymouth, Massachusetts, until 1840. The Lancaster schools had a system of training for monitors, and the academies began teacher training about 1827.

But after considerable agitation the first State normal was established through the influence of Horace Mann in 1839 at Lexington, Massachusetts. This contained a new feature for training schools in the form of a model school for the practice of students.

It would be difficult for a modern student to appreciate the opposition which Mr. Mann and his zealous colleagues met. The teaching profession as a whole considered such a movement as a reflection upon their work. But Massachusetts established three such schools within little more than a year, and the movement was successful from the beginning. The following States had established normal schools by 1860:[11] Massachusetts (three), 1839, 1840; New York, 1844; Connecticut, 1849; Michigan, 1849; Rhode Island, 1854; New Jersey, 1855; Illinois, 1857; Pennsylvania, 1859; Minnesota, 1860. It was the State normal school and teacher-training institute movement which gave John H. Vincent his inspiration for a movement to train Sunday-school teachers.

SUNDAY-SCHOOL DEVELOPMENT

The development of the Sunday school in this period may be treated under the following headings: "The Rise of the Movement," "Missionary Extension," "Typical School Organization," "Lesson Materials." The first we have already considered. The story of the spread of the Sunday-school movement over America reads like a romance. It is the story of heroic pioneers like Stephen Paxson, who braved the trackless forests, forded rivers, and suffered untold hardships in order to establish Sunday schools and circulate religious reading

---

[11] Cubberley—*Public Education in the United States*, p. 293.

matter where there were no other religious influences. It is also the story of devoted laymen, giving their time and their money unselfishly in order that boys and girls in this new land might have a chance to know about Jesus Christ and his ideals. It is the narrative of great preachers, such as Bullard, Tyng, Bushnell, and others, who, far in advance of most of the clergy of their day, saw the necessity for winning and training the child for Jesus Christ.

Missionary expansion.—The American S u n d a y - School Union placed the nation eternally in their debt by their support of Sunday-school missionaries, the preparation of lesson materials, and the circulation of inexpensive reading books before the denominations took up the work in any large way. At the sixth anniversary of the American Sunday-School Union, held in Washington Square Presbyterian Church, Philadelphia, it was resolved, "That the Union, in reliance upon divine aid, will within two years establish a Sunday school in every destitute place where it is practicable throughout the Valley of the Mississippi."[12]

The importance and difficulties of this undertaking will be better appreciated when we consider that the population of the country at this time, 1830, was approximately 13,000,000; that "Chicago was only a mud hamlet, not then having attained the dignity of a Western village, and that most of Illinois was a wild prairie or a howling wilderness."[13] Twenty-five thousand dollars was raised for this daring enterprise the first year, and sixty thousand was expended within two years. The work was heroically and successfully done

---

[12] *Experiences and Missionary Labors of Stephen Paxson*, by his daughter, B. Paxson Drury. Published by The American Sunday-School Union, 1882, p. 29.
[13] *Ibid.*, p. 30.

by Stephen Paxson and others. Many a Sunday school was planted by these intrepid pioneers where there was no other form of school and no church. The Union wisely made a great feature of its literature, and in many a frontier lonely hut and isolated community this literature proved to be an inestimable blessing.

Typical Sunday schools.—To picture an average Sunday school in any period is exceedingly difficult, and particularly so during the years which we are now considering. Clearly some of the schools, such as the one over which Mr. Pray presided as superintendent, Twelfth Congregational, Boston, or Saint George's, New York, under Dr. Tyng, were very creditable schools of religion for their day, but it is certain that on the frontiers and in many centers of population the work was very crude. There are, however, a few elements which the schools shared in common. Most of them recognized at least two departments, an infant school and a senior school, and the good ones had many classes in each. Although the Sunday school was essentially an institution for children, adults seem to have taken a great interest in it from the beginning, and very frequently throughout this period we note a demand for "special lessons for adults."

A second common element was the general curriculum material. The Bible and the catechism were universally used. In fact, the catechism was frequently employed as a means of imparting biblical instruction. It was very popular in the first one-third of this period, then waned in interest while the students applied themselves more directly to Bible study. It came back with a revival of interest in New England and other sections of the country between 1836 and 1850, but declined again. Nevertheless, in one form or another the

57

catechism has maintained a strong measure of favor as a method of religious instruction until very recent times.

A great deal of ingenuity and skill were shown in simplifying catechisms and in making them effective means for the study of Biblical history as well as Christian doctrine. Note the following excerpts from catechisms examined by the writer in the library of the American Sunday-School Union, in Philadelphia.

I. *Watts' First Catechism.* Typical questions:
   1. Can you tell me, child, who made you?
      A. The great God who made heaven and earth.

This catechism was not a study of Scripture but of scriptural doctrines.

II. *The First Catechism, by Dr. Watts. Improved Edition with Exercises.*

Contains supplementary questions on each major question as:
   1. Who made you?
   A. The great God who made heaven and earth.
      Who made heaven and earth? What is God called who made heaven and earth?

This catechism also contains a "Catechism on Scriptural Names," as well as "Prayers and Graces for Children."

III. *Watts' Second Catechism, With Proofs and Prayers.*

IV. *Historical Catechism.*

The
Abridged Bible Catechism
Arranged
In Forty Divisions
All the
Answers to the Questions
Being in the exact words of Scripture.
By W. F. Loyd, 2nd Edition, London, 1823.

V. *A Catechism—The Answers of Which Rhyme With the Questions.*

1. *Q.* Who made you, child, and bade you live?
   A. God did my life and spirit give.
   What did God give? Whose life and spirit did God give?
   Who gave you life and spirit?
2. *Q.* Who keeps you safely, can you tell?
   A. God keeps me safe and makes me well, etc.

VI.

A
Preservative
From the
Sins and Follies
of
Childhood and Youth
or
A Brief Account
of the
Sins, Vices, and Frailties
To which
Childhood and Youth Are Liable and of Which
They Should Be Warned Early.
Drawn up in the Way of
Questions and Answers,
With Arguments Against Them, Taken from
Reason and Scripture.

By Isaac Watts, D.D.,
London, 1820.

Method of study.—The main reliance in method of study was upon memorization both of the Bible and of the catechisms. Children performed the most astonishing feats of memorization, some of them having as many as hundreds of verses to their credit, for which they received as a reward tickets, or a Bible, or some good book. We read of one scholar who memorized one thousand seven hundred and fifty-two verses, of others who committed to memory the four Gospels, and it is said that most of the scholars could recite at least one hundred verses of an evening. During the latter half of this period a distinct effort was made to get away from so complete a dependence upon memorization, and to get the pupil to analyze verses, breaking them up into fragments and explaining them. Question books became a popular form of lesson material. However, it must be confessed that memorization remained the principal method of learning even where "question books" were used.

Direct Bible study.—When the tide of interest in direct Bible study began to rise the pupils were encouraged to memorize Bible verses without limit. About all that the teacher could do was to hear the verses recited and to check up the pupil for accuracy of memory. Then the leaders began to favor limiting the number of verses to be studied in a given week to a few verses in succession in the hope that this would lead the pupil to analyze each verse.

However, according to Bullard,[14] "it was found, after a short time, that many of the teachers could do but little more than hear the scholars repeat these few verses, as they used to repeat their chapters. They were not able to ask questions and interest the scholars by any instructions connected with the lesson. . . . This state of things led many to see the need of some helps and questions to be prepared by persons especially qualified for this work, on the lessons both to aid the scholars in

---

[14] Bullard—*Fifty Years with the Sabbath Schools*, pp. 52, 53. Boston, Lockwood, Brookes & Co., 1876.

studying the lessons and the teachers in imparting instruction. And this led to the preparation of question books which for many years, till the publication of the 'Uniform Lesson Papers,' most of the schools, at least in New England, have used. Indeed, most of them that use the Uniform Lessons still prefer question books to the lesson papers."

Curriculum in best schools.—Evidently, there were some schools even in this early day which selected courses to meet the needs of the various classes instead of using simply catechisms or question books. Pray[15] gives the following as "books used in Nathaniel A. Haven's School":—*Hymns for Infant Minds, Prayers Committed to Memory*, Watts' *Shorter Catechism and the Commandments*, Watts' *Historical Catechism*, Cummings' *Scripture Questions, Lessons from Scripture*, Paley's *Natural Theology*, Watts' *Improvement of the Mind* and Mason's *Self Knowledge*.

He also adds a more elaborate and perfect course of instruction which is recommended by the Sunday-School Society (Congregational).[16]

If space permitted, we would print reports of the sessions of several schools, but one may be taken as typical. The superintendent of the Congregational Sabbath school in Portsmouth, New Hampshire, the Rev. Professor Peabody, in a letter dated December 25, 1829, speaks as follows of the mode of conducting that school:

"First, prayer by the superintendent, all the children standing in one and the same attitude, and at the close, audibly joining in the Lord's Prayer. Then the class

---

[15] Pray—*History of Sunday Schools and of Religious Education from the Earliest Times*, p. 218.

[16] *Ibid.*, pp. 251, 252.

recitations. Then the superintendent relates some anecdotes, or remarks on some Scripture truth or some remarkable providence. Since requiring the children to join in the Lord's Prayer, the superintendent has usually occupied ten or fifteen minutes in illustrating and enforcing practically the several parts of it. The school is closed by singing in which all are desired to unite. Our plan has thus far succeeded admirably."[17]

The Sunday-school concert.—One of the most unique features of the Sunday schools of this period was the Sunday-school concert. This was a very popular week-night service in which the program consisted principally of prayer, brief address by the pastor or some other speaker and the reciting of Scripture verses which had been memorized. The last named feature may have accounted considerably for its popularity, for it is certain that the meetings drew crowded houses and appealed to the same interest which made the debating societies and spelling bees of this period also popular. It seems to have been very helpful in stimulating Sunday-school enthusiasm during the first half of the century.

TEACHER TRAINING

Near the close of the period there was a marked awakening of interest in teacher training, but the interest did not bring about such results as are to be noted in the next period. However, the best Sunday-school superintendents even in this early day made an effort to train their teachers. One of the books especially written for teachers and published by the American Sunday-School Union is entitled *The Teacher Taught: an Humble Attempt to Make the Path of the Teacher*

---

[17] Bullard—*Fifty Years with the Sabbath Schools*, pp. 53, 54.

Straight and Plain. This book (page 209) says, "It was a prominent feature of the plan to organize the officers and teachers of the school into a class to be conducted by the pastor of the church (if any) to which the school belonged, and to gain from him and from mutual conferences a full knowledge of the subject of instruction."

Sunday-school aims.—The central aim of the Sunday-school leaders of this period is easily discovered. The Rev. Stephen H. Tyng, rector of Saint George's Church, New York, writing in 1860 and looking back over forty years of experience, says, "You will see that this whole train of remark is founded upon my previous assertion of the purpose of Sunday-school teaching—that it is the actual conversion of children to God."[18]

Many similar quotations could be given. The ideal of training for effective Christian service in this life was not entirely forgotten, but it was overshadowed by the other purpose. It must have been held by many, either consciously or unconsciously, that if the individual once "got right with God," divine guidance would protect and inspire him through the journey of life without much assistance from teachers. The amount of attention given to preparing the child for death is bewildering to the student of to-day. The children's story papers featured deathbed scenes. Examples of children who wanted to die and "be in the arms of Jesus" are frequently brought to the attention of the young readers.

We may say that the dominant ideal of this period was conversion and that a secondary ideal was knowledge of the subject matter of the Bible. One cannot escape

[18] Tyng—*Forty Years' Experience in Sunday Schools,* pp. 89, 90.

the conviction that Bible verses in the minds of young
scholars were expected to work like magic by bringing
about conversion whether the pupil understood their
meaning or not. Naturally, there were frequent protests against the cramming of unexplained verses and
catechism answers into young minds, but the prevailing
practice at least until near the end of the period over-
ruled these protests. Many Bible stories and verses are
so simple that they will carry their own message, and
the mere memorization of these by pupils whose teachers
are incompetent will accomplish good, but neither the
aims nor the methods of this period were adequate.
We do not minimize the great achievements of these
heroic, devoted workers when we cite the limitations
under which they labored.

SUMMARY

This chapter has attempted to trace briefly the rise
of the Sunday-school movement in America after
receiving its initial impulse from Robert Raikes in
England. That it peculiarly fitted the needs of this
new land and spread rapidly across the frontier as well
as in centers of habitation is a matter of record. We
have noted the gradual development of a national
system of free, tax-supported, State-controlled public
schools which eliminated both the Bible and all other
definite religious materials from its curriculum. We
have noted the progress toward perfecting this public-
school system, especially the movement in State normal
schools to prepare teachers. And, finally, we have tried
to glimpse the growing Sunday-school movement, noting
typical cases of school method and of curriculum together with typical statements of the aims of Sunday-

school education for this period. On the whole this was a period of great expansion of Sunday-school interest. The perfection of the materials and methods of these schools is the task of a later day but great credit must be given to these pioneers of the first half of the nineteenth century who laid so well the foundations of religious instruction in a day when the nation was perfecting a system of general education without the use of religious materials.

Questions for discussion:

1. What were the most significant achievements of the Sunday-school leaders of the first half of the nineteenth century?

2 Investigate further the development of the public-school system during this period in its several aspects such as (a) organization and administration, (b) curriculum, (c) teacher training.

3. To what extent did the system of Sunday-school instruction keep pace with the system of public-school instruction?

4. Investigate and describe types of Sunday schools of this period in (a) New England, (b) New York, Philadelphia, (c) the Western frontier.

5. Estimate the value to the nation of the services rendered by the frontier missionaries of the American Sunday-School Union.

6. Estimate the value of the services rendered by the American Sunday-School Union in the circulation of good literature.

7. What do you think were the aims of the Sunday-school leaders of this period—to what extent were they adequate?

8. Of what value was the Sunday-school concert?

9. To what extent were Sunday-school teachers being trained?

Brief bibliography of selected reference:

Harris—*Robert Raikes: The Man and His Work.* E. P. Dutton & Company, New York, 1899.

Watson—*The First Fifty Years of the Sunday School.* Sunday-School Union, London, n. d.

Rice—*The Sunday-School Movement and the American Sunday-School Union, 1780–1917.* The American Sunday-School Union, Philadelphia, 1917.

Pray—*The History of Sunday Schools and of Religious Education from the Earliest Times.* William Crosby and H. P. Nichols, Boston, 1847.

Bullard—*Fifty Years With the Sabbath Schools.* Lockwood, Brookes & Company, 1876.

Tyng—*Forty Years' Experience in Sunday Schools.* Sheldon and Company, New York, 1860.

Drury, B. Paxson—*Experiences and Labors of Stephen Paxson.* The American Sunday-School Union, Philadelphia, 1882.

Wardle—*History of the Sunday-School Movement in the Methodist Episcopal Church.* The Methodist Book Concern, New York, 1918.

Brown—*Sunday-School Movements in America.* Fleming H. Revell, New York, 1901.

Cubberley—*Public Education in the United States.* Houghton Mifflin Company, Boston, 1919.

Brown—*The Making of Our Middle Schools.* Longmans, Green and Co., New York, 1918.

Dexter—*History of Education in the United States.* The Macmillan Company, New York, 1919.

CHAPTER IV

THE SUNDAY SCHOOLS FROM 1860-1900

THE first half of the period which we are about to discuss would be described by many as the most significant period in all Sunday-school history. It was featured by the leadership of remarkable men, and the movements inaugurated by them had far-reaching influence not only in the field of religious education, but also in the field of general popular education.

A great war such as the Civil War in America, or the recent World War, may always be expected to awaken a new interest in religious education. The foundations of society are shaken by such a catastrophe, the passions of men are at their worst. Hatred, murder, pillage, and lust are the inevitable accompaniments of war, even though the soldiers have high ideals for their own nations and sacrifice themselves for these ideals nobly. But a war jars people from their complacency. To rebuild a devastated world nations must first restore morale, rebuild human character for better achievement. Facing such a problem, emphasis upon religious education is inevitable. This was precisely the case in 1865 and the years immediately following, as it was in America immediately after the year 1918.

However, Sunday-school progress would seem to have been inevitable even if there had been no war. The National Convention of 1859 indicated that the growth of Sunday-school interest had been rapid and widespread. The finally complete divorcement of public-school education from religious education made the church turn its attention to this as its one best opportunity to teach religion to the young. And the normal-school movement which had swept over the country and was producing results of the most gratifying significance was certain to be felt sooner or later in a movement for the normal training of Sunday-school teachers.

The fact is that the first twenty years of this period mark one of the most significant epochs in the history of religious education. The articles appearing in the religious periodicals of this period give evidence that the air was electric with anticipation and confidence. For the writers a new day had dawned in Christian progress. The Bible was to be studied as never before, teachers were to be made competent, colleges and seminaries were to cooperate actively in the preparation of Sunday-school teachers.

To see to what extent these high hopes were realized will be the task of the student of this chapter. Much was done and much was left for a later generation to do. We will seek to discover how much the leaders actually accomplished in this period, to what extent they may have failed, and what were the net results of their achievements.

ADVANCE BEGINS WITH TEACHER TRAINING

Probably no factor is more responsible for the success of the movement in this era than the great interest in teacher training which ushered in the period and made many of the later developments possible. The success of the State normal schools and the State and county teachers' institutes had overcome all opposition to normal training and clearly made possible a new day in public-school education. The significance of this movement profoundly impressed the Sunday-school leaders. During the first half of the century able leaders had pleaded for the training of Sunday-school teachers, a few books and pamphlets had been written to assist in such training, and some of the good schools had maintained successful teachers' meetings. The Rev. D. P. Kidder, corresponding secretary of the Sunday-School Union of the Methodist Episcopal Church, suggested in 1847 that the church use the method of teachers' institutes which was proving so helpful to public-school teachers. He urged the formation of "Normal Sunday Schools," and in 1848 his book, *The Sunday-School Teachers' Guide*, was published. However, in that year while urging the formation of training classes, he said, "We confess, however, that we fear the day is distant when the church will take as high ground on this subject as that already assumed by several States of this Union."[1]

But sentiment was being created along this line, and when John H. Vincent, in 1860, presented the report of the Conference Sunday-School Committee to the Rock River Conference, held in Chicago, the report contained the following suggestions: "The importance of teachers' institutes to the educational interest of our country cannot have escaped your attention. May we not profitably introduce something similar among us? Such an institute conducted by our ablest Sunday-school educators could not fail to elevate our standard and improve our system of religious culture." The report was unanimously adopted by the Conference.

Mr. Vincent was a young Methodist preacher who already had behind him several years of experience as

---

[1] *Annual Report of the Sunday-School Union of the Methodist Episcopal Church,* Report of 1848, p. 99.

the teacher of a "normal class." The response of his colleagues in the Conference was hearty, and during the next few years he held numerous successful institutes. Allied with him in the vicinity of Chicago were a number of young men, such as B. F. Jacobs, Edward Eggleston, and others, who were zealous promoters of improved methods of Sunday-school work. In the East at about the same time Mr. R. G. Pardee and Mr. Ralph Wells began also to organize institutes, so that within ten years after the first Illinois Sunday-School Teachers' Institute had held its session the plan had been widely adopted throughout the United States.

A great forward step.—Undoubtedly this w i d e - spread interest in teacher training and the improvement in Sunday-school methods resulting therefrom made possible what some have called "the greatest single step ever taken by the Sunday school"—the creation of a system of International Uniform Sunday School Lessons. These lessons were the direct result of the efforts of B. F. Jacobs, a layman of Chicago, and John H. Vincent, made possible through the growing popularity of national and international Sunday-school conventions.

NATIONAL SUNDAY-SCHOOL CONVENTIONS

The earliest national conventions were convened in 1832, 1833, and 1859, all being held in Philadelphia. The Fourth National Convention was held in Newark, New Jersey, in 1869, and the Fifth National Convention in Indianapolis, April 16–19, 1872.

Fortunately, the Sunday-school movement has never been narrowly sectarian. The present type of the movement received its initial impulse from a layman, Robert Raikes, and the early organizations in America for the promotion of it were composed largely of laymen.

Clergymen, however, have been very influential in promoting the work. Such names as Wesley, Tyng, Bullard, Vincent, and Blackall will indicate how much they have done to promote and guide Sunday-school development. Nevertheless, it has not been until very recent years that the churches officially through their ministers have become such powerful factors in controlling its destinies as they are to-day.

The great Conventions were essentially for laymen, worked up by laymen with the aid of a few outstanding ministers who had a passion for Sunday-school work. The fact that laymen are not so interested in sectarian propaganda as ministers and the fact that laymen were the controlling force in Sunday-school conventions may account in part for the action in 1872. After careful deliberation, and almost unanimously, the International Sunday-School Convention of 1872 created an International Lesson Committee and recommended that this committee select and organize lesson materials for one uniform Bible lesson to be used throughout the world by pupils of all ages. B. F. Jacobs, of Illinois, a layman with a genius for organization and a passion for Sunday-school work, pushed the plan most vigorously supported by John H. Vincent. Edward Eggleston and a few with him opposed the scheme, in part because they favored graded lesson materials instead of a uniform lesson, and in part because they opposed the particular type of lesson which they thought would be in the ascendancy under the leadership of Dr. Vincent.

The International Lesson System.—It was much easier to persuade the convention to adopt the plan than to persuade the denominations to accept it. The leading denominations were printing their own lessons with appropriate helps and had a great deal of money

71

invested in plates which would become worthless under the new scheme. It is a great tribute to the unselfishness and zeal of the churches that they were willing to surrender their advantages, forget their differences of opinion, and embark upon a common enterprise for the spread of biblical knowledge. This expression of so nearly a united Protestantism in an effort to win and develop the young in the Christian faith started an era of unprecedented advance in Sunday-school growth. A more detailed study of this lesson system and the work of the International Lesson Committee will be found in the following chapter. At this point we are chiefly concerned with the creation of the system and with some of the results which followed.

International Sunday-School Conventions.—From this time on the conventions were called international conventions, and were held regularly, one every three years until 1914, when the interval was changed to four years. Intense interest and enthusiasm have marked the meetings. Occasionally the differences over methods and materials have caused sharp debates, but the zeal for a common cause has preserved the spirit of unity in a remarkable way. The International Lesson Committee was elected once every six years, and its basis of organization remained unchanged until 1914. The lessons which they recommended passed through relatively only minor modifications until the International Convention of 1908 authorized the Lesson Committee to issue not only outlines for uniform lessons, but also for graded lessons.

AIMS AND IDEALS OF THE PERIOD

What were the aims and ideals of the Sunday-school movement in this period? Clearly the supreme aim was conversion, the winning of new recruits for Jesus Christ. As a secondary aim he was to be won through Bible study, his faith was to be established through Bible study, and his growth in Christian character together with his usefulness as a Christian in the church and community was to be brought about essentially through Bible study.

To be sure, many phrases can be found indicating a feeling after the idea of training through actual service, and a recognition of the importance of church history, missionary and other materials to prepare the Christian for useful service; but so far as the Sunday school itself is concerned, this feeling during this period never found expression in any modification of lesson material through the International Lesson Committee, or in any adaptation of program authorized by an international convention. The workers were willing that other agencies, such as the Society of Christian Endeavor and the Epworth League, should supplement the Sunday school, and did not modify their program so that the Sunday school itself could meet these other needs.

The Report of the Proceedings of the General Sunday-School Convention held in London, September 1–5 inclusive, 1862, is illuminating on this point. The report states that the composition of the convention was as follows: "Forty-eight were officers or members of the Committee; 19, chairmen or others taking part in the proceedings of the convention; 13, Foreign delegates; 193, Country delegates; 85, London delegates; 38, ministers; and 37, visitors."[2] The United States, Australia, Canada, France, Italy, and Switzerland sent

---

[2] *The Report of the Proceedings of the General Sunday-School Convention,* held in London, September 1st, 2d, 3d, 4th, and 5th, 1862. Fourth Edition. Published by Sunday-School Union, 5 Old Bailey, London, E.C., p. V.

delegates, the United States being represented by the
Rev. William M. Blackburn, the Rev. C. W. Bolton,
W. C. Chapin, Esq., the Rev. F. S. DeHass, the Rev.
Dr. McClintock, the Rev. J. H. Vincent, and A. Wood-
ruff, Esq.

The report of the meetings is exceedingly significant
because in very frank discussions these leaders were
seeking to obtain the facts concerning the exact Sunday-
school situation in the countries represented and to
come to agreement so far as possible with respect to
aims and methods of Sunday-school promotion.

On the second day of the convention Mr. Charles
Reed read a paper on "The Great Object of Sunday-
School Teaching." In the course of his paper he said,
"For a religious education to be worth the name it must
regard the soul: 'first see that the spirit is safe for
heaven, and then let us teach how to spend the intervening time on earth.' Let the week attend to the
things of the week: once regard the great aim to be
conversion, and the Sabbath will be redeemed for holy
duties and spiritual husbandry."[3] Later in the same
paper he says, "Brethren, if these things be so, then
let us lay our account to this—We are bound to seek
conversion as our great aim; bound by every obligation
to our God, to the parent, to the child, to our own
conscience."[4]

"After the discussion of the subject by others, Mr.
Reed in closing the conversation, said if there had not
been much discussion, it was because there was almost
perfect unanimity. The subject did not need discussion, for happily no issue had been raised. No one had
attacked the principle which he had laid down; it was

---

[3] Report, p. 52.
[4] Report, p. 55.

accepted as settled. . . . 'What are the chief needs in the Sunday-school in the present day?' He would say, 'Spiritual-mindedness in our teachers, and separate accommodation for our senior scholars.' "[5]

It seems clear to the writer that, while the forward-looking Sunday-school leaders knew that conversion was only the beginning of the process of developing a holy life, they were so overwhelmed by a sense of the need of conversion on the part of multitudes that they were willing to leave the development of the converts to other agencies such as pastors' or confirmation classes. Many phrases to the contrary may be quoted, but a careful reading of the discussions will show much more attention to the subject of how to win converts than to the subject of training the convert after he has been won so that he can go out and help others. That many teachers were indifferent to the aim, and poorly qualified to achieve it, is recognized, also that the leaders had no fixed type of emotional or intellectual experience in mind as a goal, but the principal aim—conversion—was an all-absorbing one.

The selection of curriculum material must be considered in the light of this purpose. If conversion was the supreme task, then the Bible alone supplied sufficient study material. But if the development of the young Christian for his Christian duties had also been an aim, then in the nature of the case, church history, fundamental doctrines, missionary achievements, and other materials would have been recognized as necessary. They were at this time recognized as useful but not as proper materials for Sunday study and hence left to other agencies. It was not until near the end of this

---

Report, p. 66.

period that any considerable demand for extra-biblical material in the Sunday-school curriculum arose.

Classification of scholars.—Let us try to picture typical Sunday schools. The convention in London also took up for discussion the question of Sunday-school classification, following a paper on this subject by Mr. R. W. Collins. Mr. Collins said, "Separate the scholars into four parts, and call these divisions, not 'classes'—the Infant, Elementary, Scripture, and Senior Divisions."[6] He further recommended:

1. Infant Division to be strictly infants. Sixty or more can be efficiently managed by one teacher and an assistant.

2. The Elementary Division will comprise those who can read but not fluently. Eight to twelve may be in a class.

3. The Scripture Division will include all those scholars who can read the Scriptures. Eight to twelve may be in classes.

4. The Senior Division will comprehend those scholars who are above the age of fourteen. Fifteen to twenty may be in the classes.

Dr. Vincent said in the discussion that in an ideal school other departments should be added. He said in part:

"Here are the infant scholars, and for these he has the Infant Division; here are the elementary scholars, and for these he has a division; so with the Scripture and Senior Divisions. But each school should provide in some way for its own supply of teachers. Where is the Normal or Training Division? To teach the Bible effectually there should be a careful study of archæology and geography, in a systematic way, but this cannot be done on the Sabbath day without interfering with the

---

[6] *Report of General Sunday-School Convention*, 1862, p. 74.

religious and practical part of teaching. Some schools in America have an archæological division and week-day meetings. I have one in my school and call it the 'Palestine Class.' Then we want to bring the children and youth to the Saviour and bring them under direct pastoral influence. There ought in every church to be an 'Inquirers' Division,' a 'probationers' or a 'converts' class. This is the better and more perfect division:— Infant, Elementary, Scripture, Senior, Normal, Archæological, and Inquirers' Division."[7]

Dr. Vincent was successful in introducing normal divisions in many schools, but the Archæological and Inquirers' divisions never figured very vitally as Sunday-school organizations. The study of archæology formed a very interesting feature of the work of the normal classes, but the "Palestine Clubs" as such did not hold their popularity long. The Inquirers' Division was more commonly conducted as an independent organization directed by the pastor. Pardee, writing in 1869, offers and answers the following question: "Would you recommend the grading of Sabbath schools? We like the word 'adaptation,' for there must be *that* in all good teaching; there must also be acknowledgment and thorough Bible instruction. But we fear that an attempt to grade Sunday schools would stiffen and injure them, for we have but one hour in a week, while the public schools have six hours per day and five days in a week, with a dozen grades of textbooks and paid diciplined teachers. Besides, we have never found a successful Sabbath school with more than three regular grades, viz: the infants class, the intermediate classes, and the young men and women classes."[8]

---

[7] *Report of General Sunday-School Convention*, 1862, p. 84.

[8] Pardee—*The Sabbath-School Index*, pp. 241, 242.

Later titles of divisions.—Toward the end of this period the titles of the divisions underwent the following changes:

Infant—Kindergarten and Beginners.
Elementary—Primary.
Scripture—Juniors.
Senior—Everything above Junior.

The title "infants' class" still persists in backward schools, and until very recently in many places comprehended all children under twelve or fourteen, while the word "senior" indicated everyone older. By 1890 many good schools recognized the following classification:

Beginners or Kindergarten—Up to five inclusive.
Primary—Six to eight (often ten).
Junior—Nine to twelve.
Intermediate—Thirteen to sixteen or eighteen.

Large schools would have several classes and small schools would have only one class to a division.

Architecture.—The aims of the Sunday schools of this period were expressed also in the architecture of their rooms or buildings. Even down to the present many churches have no housing accommodations especially planned for the Sunday school. But in 1867 a building was designed which seemed to be ideal. It was designed by Lewis Miller, inventor of the Buckeye Mower and Reaper, in consultation with John H. Vincent, and the plan of this Sunday-school building in Akron has ever since been known as the Akron plan. Until recent years the plan was accepted as a standard by leading Sunday-school workers, and even to this day, although now disapproved by most Sunday-school leaders, it is still the pattern to some extent of many buildings designed for Sunday-school use.

It provided for the separate divisions and for class-rooms within the division sections, and also for a common assembly of old and young when the partitions were pushed out of the way. This building seemed to be admirably suited to the two outstanding aims of the school of this period—conversion and a particular type of Bible study. The common assembly, with its lively music and the stirring address of a superintendent, pastor, or outside speaker, might be effective in persuading pupils to begin the Christian life. It also afforded a good opportunity for Bible drills. But it could not be used to teach little children how to pray, or how to understand the meaning of hymns. It clearly was not suitable for training them in worship. The class stalls, or "cubby holes," were a real help to teachers in that they gave to the classes a certain amount of privacy. But the general plan erred because it cut up into little rooms much space which might more properly have been used for departmental worship.

Teaching methods.—One of the interesting problems for a student of history is to note how certain movements and methods prove to meet a real need in one age and in a succeeding generation become a positive handicap. There is no doubt but that the Sunday-school movement from 1860 to 1890 was a vitally successful teaching movement. It had many imperfections, but it was promoted throughout the land by men and women burning with zeal to win the young for Christ and to see the new recruits taken into the church. These faithful workers also had a passion for biblical knowledge. The battles between science and religion, or, to be more accurate, between many of the adherents of science and of the adherents of Christianity were raging. Battles were also fiercely fought between the

men who had adopted the scientific critical methods of
Bible study and the conservative champions of the Bible
stories as they had always known them.

Certainly, through at least two thirds of the period
it was a popular mass movement in Bible study. The
questions suggested in the lesson helps led to interesting
discussions if the teachers were at all competent, and
literally thousands of teachers were studying diligently
to make themselves competent. Great weekly teachers'
meetings were not uncommon, some of them having
hundreds, even as high as eighteen hundred in regular
attendance.[9]

But as an educational movement it deteriorated in
the "nineties." Thousands continued to study and
individual schools improved, but the passion for Bible
study and for securing conversions waned. Although
the lesson quarterlies had never been better they did
not lead to popular Bible study. Teachers prepared their
lessons hastily, if at all, and the asking of questions from
the printed page of the quarterly became in many places
as dead a performance as the asking of questions out of
a catechism had come to be in 1830.

**Influence of Pestalozzi, Froebel, and Herbart
through the public schools.**—Besides, teaching methods and materials in the public-school world were
improving rapidly. The methods and theories of
Pestalozzi, Froebel, and Herbart had been imported
from overseas and were revolutionizing public-school
policies. Formal instruction for its disciplinary value
was giving place to an effort to teach only "knowledge
that was worth while." The public school pupil was
beginning to study reading, arithmetic, and geography

---

[9] Tompkins Avenue Congregational Church, Brooklyn, under the leadership
of Robert Meredith.

in terms of his own immediate interests and problems. The new science of psychology referred to in the early part of this period in a vague way as "mental science" was beginning to furnish accurate data as to just what materials and methods were useful for developing the mind in the different periods of its growth.

The public-school world made no great haste to accept the newer educational methods, but by 1890 some of these principles had been accepted long enough to prove their merit. This movement had its effect upon popular approval of the Sunday school and upon the younger leaders of the Sunday school. The school of religion suffered as never before in comparison with public-school efficiency.

Pioneers in reform.—The "infant-class" workers of Newark and New York city as far back as 1871 began to promote the use of special lessons for their classes, and in 1884 the National Primary Union was formed, changing its name in 1887 to the International Primary Union of the United States and British Provinces. They early tried to secure a modification of the International Uniform Lessons in their favor. About 1890 the Rev. Erastus Blakeslee, backed by William Rainey Harper, then of Yale University, and others began to publish graded lesson materials. These materials were all biblical, but the preparation of them, assisted by judicious advertising, had great effect upon the agitation for an improved lesson system.

Beginnings of new experimentation.—Great interest in the Sunday school remained despite opposition to its methods and the form of its lesson materials. Nevertheless, from 1890 to 1910 the Sunday-school movement found itself in an era of conflict, of experimentation, of arrested growth, in contrast with the epochs immediately preceding and immediately following. In order to understand the era of conflict and experimentation we must go back and review the developments in curricula and teacher training of the preceding one hundred years, and especially of the preceding half a century.

SUMMARY

We have noted in this chapter an era of great progress. This progress was ushered in by an awakening to religious educational needs produced by the Civil War, and was greatly stimulated by a nation-wide interest in teacher training, both secular and religious. We have noted the growing popularity of great international conventions and the epochal achievement of promoting one lesson system for the greater part of the Protestant world through the newly formed International Lesson Committee. We have studied briefly the aims of the period and how they found expression in the curriculum, and in the provisions for housing the school. The success of the movement until the late eighties we have seen to be wonderful. Then we found ourselves entering not upon a period of decline but of arrested development because of demands for changes in methods and materials.

The galaxy of great men like Jacobs, Vincent, Eggleston, Trumbull, Schauffler, Hurlbut, and a host of others who helped to build a great system of religious instruction have left the world eternally in their debt. The next generation modified their methods, but they built upon a foundation well laid by able, faithful men. These successors had little to undo but much unfinished work to accomplish. They were no more radical or progressive for their day than the leaders who pioneered for a world-wide study of a common Bible passage on a given Sunday were in their day. To trace the work of the next generation of builders will be the principal task of the remaining chapters.

Success and failure.—The student of history who is trying to estimate the successes and failures of this period will undoubtedly credit these leaders with the creation of a system of religious education which saved the nation to a large extent from the perils of atheism and materialism. As Dr. Vincent frequently said, "The Sunday school is strong at the heart and weak at the head." No one recognized better than he the necessity for better teaching, and no one ever worked harder to secure such. At the same time, if the estimation of E. Payson Porter[10] in 1887 of one million teachers and eight million scholars for the United States alone is correct, and if the Sunday school of this era was effective at the heart, in motivation—as we believe it was—the student may form some reasonable estimate of the success of this imperfect institution.

A commission was sent over by the French government in 1876 and Dr. Trumbull tells us that it was evident in the voluminous report prepared by Monsieur F. Buisson, the president of the commission, that "no department of primary education had impressed that careful observer as more important and more noteworthy than that of the Sunday school."[11] "The Sunday school," he said, "is not an accessory agency in the normal economy of American education; it does not add a superfluity; it is an absolute necessity for the complete instruction of the child. Its aim is to fill by itself the complex mission which elsewhere

---

[10] Trumbull—*Yale Lectures on the Sunday School*, p. 133. Copyrighted by Estate of Henry Clay Trumbull. Publishing rights owned by Charles Scribner's Sons. Used by permission.

[11] *Ibid.*, p. 132.

is in a large measure assigned to the family, the school, and the church."[12]

If one were asked to name the one outstanding failure of these great leaders, he would say that they, like other educators, did not sufficiently understand child nature nor adequately appreciate the unity of the educational process. Perhaps they were as far along as the rank and file of leaders in general education of their day, but it is difficult to excuse an analysis of child life and educational processes which assigns to one agency "enlistment," or the establishing of right motives, to another the imparting of information, and to a third "drill," as does the great scholar, Dr. Trumbull. "The threefold work of winning, improving, and of exercising— of enlistment, of instruction, and of drill—must proceed wherever the training process is made practical, to the completion of the religious life of young disciples of Christ to-day. The first factor in this work we may say is represented by the pulpit; the second, by the Sunday school; the third, by the auxiliary agencies of guilds, and boards, and associations, and societies, and orders, and leagues, and circles for the prosecution of particular lines of effort, or for the cultivation of particular virtues, which for lack of a better name may be counted as the 'gymnasia' of the church (using that term in its classical signification) in which the young membership is to have practice in moral and spiritual athletics."[13]

Of course the above statement is not offered by Dr. Trumbull as a clean-cut analysis, but it is typical of the prevailing opinion of the time which encouraged the organization of the Society of Christian Endeavor,

---

[12] Trumbull—*Yale Lectures on the Sunday School*, p. 132. Copyrighted by Estate of Henry Clay Trumbull. Publishing rights owned by Charles Scribner's Sons. Used by permission.

[13] *Ibid.*, p. 283.

1881, to take care of the expressional aspects of education while the Sunday school confined itself to the imparting of biblical information and the efforts to secure "conversions" (establishing of right motives). The Sunday-school leaders did undertake two of the aspects of education; but if they had accepted responsibility for the third, broadening their curriculum materials so as to make their training for Christian living more effective, they would have set forward the cause of Christian education by at least half a century.

Questions for discussion:

1. To what extent was the new interest in religious education noted at the beginning of the period due to the Civil War?

2. To what extent was the awakening due to the teacher-training movement that was in progress when the war began?

3. Do you believe this era of advance would have come approximately when it did if there had been no such war?

4. Discuss the merits and defects of the International Uniform Lesson system from the standpoint of conditions in 1872. Was it the best possible system for that day?

5. How long did the passion for Bible study noted in this period last? What were the permanent effects of this enthusiastic movement?

6. What were the principal achievements of Sunday-school leaders from 1870 to 1890? What failures, if any, should be noted?

7. So far as you can estimate it, what were the prevailing types of piety or Christian experience produced by the Sunday-school system of this

period? To what extent were these types adequate for their day? To what extent would they be adequate for the present day?

8. Was the organization of young people's societies as organizations independent of the Sunday school a detriment or a help to the cause of religious education?

9. What was the net contribution of this period to the cause of religious education?

Brief bibliography of selected references:

Trumbull—*Yale Lectures on the Sunday School.* Charles Scribner's Sons, New York, 1904. (Copyright, 1888.)

Report of the Proceedings of the General Sunday-School Convention, held in London September 1–5, 1862. Published by Sunday-School Union, 5 Old Bailey, London.

Vincent—*The Modern Sunday School.* Phillips and Hunt, New York, 1887.

Vincent—*The Church School, and Normal Guide.* Hunt and Eaton, New York, 1889.

Pardee—*The Sabbath-School Index.* J. C. Garrigues & Co., Philadelphia, 1869.

Sampey—*The International Lesson System.* The Sunday-School Board of the Southern Baptist Convention, Nashville, Tenn., and Fleming H. Revell Company, New York, 1911.

Files of the Denominational Sunday-school periodicals for this period.

International Sunday-School Association—*Reports of Conventions.*

CHAPTER V

THE DEVELOPMENT OF SUNDAY-SCHOOL CURRICULA

THE curriculum is the lesson material through which an educational institution seeks to accomplish its aims. In any period the curriculum is apt to be found in a fluid state, as it should be. Experiments are always being conducted by any efficient educational system. The curriculum materials are first tested while in temporary mold and then gradually are cast into permanent textbook form. But by the time the materials have been put into book form some of the most progressive educators will have found success with new methods and materials, so that the textbooks will be out of date for the leaders by the time that they are in print.

THE CURRICULUM ALWAYS CHANGING

The curriculum simply will not "stay put." For this reason some teachers object to the organization of curriculum materials into any form which may appear to be fixed and inelastic for even a brief period. They prefer to have the teachers develop their own curriculum to meet the needs of the changing social environment in which the pupil lives. On the other hand, many who believe thoroughly in the necessity of keeping the curriculum in a fluid state feel that only a genius can hope to organize his own material to meet the needs of his pupils, and that for the average teacher the best teaching experience of others should be put into convenient form for his use. The latter are still the dominant group in education, but it is doubtful how long they may retain their supremacy. All realize that a textbook in history or in science is apt to be out of date as soon as it is written, but they also recognize that it may serve to bring others up to the line while the scouting parties in educational fields go further ahead.

The hardest problem for the teacher is to find the material which presents the truth as he wishes to have it presented in the light of his most recent investigations. In practice he will take the best books he can find and supplement these with the latest material that he has discovered. With these facts of general experience in mind we will expect to find the curriculum of every period changing. When it ceases to change we can be sure of stagnation and not progress.

Generally speaking, we have divided this history into four periods: The colonial period, the years 1784-1860; the years 1860-1900; and from 1900 to the present.

Curriculum of the colonial period.—In the colonial period the principal curriculum material was biblical in one form or another. Whether the verses and prayers were in the *Hornbook*, the *Primer*, the *Speller*, the *Catechism*, or the Bible itself, the materials were essentially religious. It is clear that they were selected to influence conduct in this life, and to prepare one for death. They were a collection of the materials considered most essential to fit the pupil for his duties as a Christian citizen. We have already described the contents of the *Hornbook* and of the *New England Primer*.[1] We have also noted the gradual secularization of the common-school curriculum beginning with the intro-

[1] See Chapter II.

88

duction of Dillworth's *A New Guide to the English Tongue*, and Webster's *American Spelling Book*. From this time on more and more of secular material was introduced into the curriculum of the common schools, gradually crowding out the biblical, until as early as the days of Horace Mann it was a question whether the Bible should even be read devotionally in the public schools. Horace Mann himself favored reading the Bible without comment, but he did not favor teaching it.

CHAOTIC STATE OF CURRICULUM—1784–1860

The condition of the curriculum from 1784 to 1860 may well be called chaotic. Sampey speaks of the last thirty years of this period as a period when the "so-called 'Babel Series' held sway."[2] But there was considerable of "Babel" during the earlier part of the period as well. So long as the *Primer* and the *Catechism* were dominant the lesson material was definite. But in breaking away from these formal materials the Sunday-school world fell into much confusion. For a time the practice seems to have been to permit the pupil to learn as many Bible verses as he could memorize and to select them from any part of the Bible whatsoever. Then the definite effort was made to confine the lesson to a limited portion of the Scriptures, but in this case the lessons were selected at random and the chief task of the teacher was to hear the pupils recite verses from memory.

If the pupils of a Sunday school needed it, a speller might be used as curriculum material. The catechism seems to have made a strong bid for popularity, for the

---

[2] Sampey—*The International Lesson System*, p. 37. The Sunday-School Board of the Southern Baptist Convention and Fleming H. Revell Company, publishers. Used by permission.

library of the American Sunday-School Union contains many catechisms, some very ingenious, published between 1800 and 1830. In the early thirties there was a revival in New England of enthusiasm for the catechism, but a revival very vigorously opposed by some. A very interesting book on the subject published by J. Leavitt, of New York, and Crocker and Brewster, Boston, 1831, contains a very instructive protest against the prevailing method of simply memorizing a catechism. The title page gives the following:

The
End and Essence
of
Sabbath School Teaching
and
Family Religious Instruction
in Which
The Present Defects in Communicating
Religious Knowledge to the Young
Are Investigated
and
The Lesson System
of
Teaching the Scriptures
is
Fully Developed.

"I had rather speak five words with my *understanding* that by my voice I might teach others also, than ten thousand words in an unknown tongue."—1 Cor. XIV: 19.

Significant progress.—However, the most significant and most orderly curriculum development seems to have been as follows: In 1824, the *Sunday-School Teachers' Magazine*, of London, suggested that it would be a wiser practice to assign certain portions of Scripture and Catechism, instead of letting the children select and commit what they pleased. In October of the same year "The New York Association of Sunday-School Teachers" passed a resolution declaring that "all lessons in Sabbath Schools should be selected," and on January 1, 1825, they commenced a series of selected lessons for the four following months.

The American Sunday-School Union at once espoused the new idea, and in March, 1825, published a card containing a list of forty-nine lessons for one year, according to Dr. Sampey, divided into four parts, so as to leave room for a quarterly examination of the scholars. The lessons were used in many schools in New York, Philadelphia, and other cities in 1825. The experiment was so successful that, in response to many requests, the trial list was carefully revised and issued for general use for one year, from May, 1826, to May, 1827."[3]

The Rev. Albert Judson was employed by the New York Sunday-School Union to prepare for teachers a series of questions *of three grades* on the lessons, and the demand for these questions issued in pamphlet form greatly exceeded the supply. Dr. Rice says of these questions: "Judson's questions were of three grades. The first grade consisted of such plain and easy questions as might be answered by citing some clause of the Bible text. The second grade comprised less simple questions, calling for more thought and leading the teacher to explain, and the scholar to know the meaning of the text. The third grade of questions were those which arose from the subject of study and from the passage of Scripture where the same or a like

_____

[3] Sampey—*The International Lesson System*, p. 23.

topic was taught. This called for a more general study of Scripture to discover how the same truth was presented by different sacred writers."[4]

This improvement in lesson materials led to a revival of interest in Bible study and in Sunday-school work generally. Rival systems were merged into one by the Sunday-School Union, which issued "Union Questions" in several volumes. Dr. Sampey says of this development, "Had there been a strong permanent Lesson Committee, representative of the leading evangelical denominations, it would seem that the great movement of 1872 might have been anticipated by more than forty years."[5]

Union Questions, Volume I, "Containing the History of the Life of Jesus Christ" (American Sunday-School Union, 1834), says in the preface: "The excellence of the system of instruction on which *Union Questions* are founded is now so universally admitted that there is no reason for detailing its advantages. The first volume was published by the American Sunday-School Union in 1827, and many large editions have been circulated."[6] Volumes III and IV (combined) state the following: "The great object of a book of questions is to excite the mind to a careful and thorough examination of the Scriptures."[7]

It appears that very useful lesson helps were prepared to assist the teachers in the use of these lesson materials, but no adequate provision was made for the needs of the pupils. In time *Union Questions* grew into a series of nine years' studies; four years being given to the New Testament and five to the Old Testament.

4 Rice—Important and Remarkable Epochs in the History of Sunday Schools, pp. 10–11. The American Sunday-School Union, publishers. Used by permission.
5 Sampey—*The International Lesson System*, p. 27.
6 Used by permission of the American Sunday-School Union.
7 *Ibid.*

"Verse-a-Day System a Handicap."—The movement just described marked progress along the right line, but it is surprising to note that just when the better system was well under way a retrograde movement came in, known as "The Verse-a-Day Scheme." It may not have been the intention of many for this plan to supplant the "Selected Lessons," but its growing popularity for a time did set back the movement for better lesson materials by its reemphasis upon verse memorization instead of more effective teaching.

Influence of denominational unions and publishing houses.—But after about 1830 the denominational unions and publishing houses began to challenge the supremacy of the publications of the American Sunday-School Union and to issue their own lesson schemes. This led to what has been called "The Babel Series," because a visitor from one Sunday school to another might find a different passage of Scripture used as the lesson in each school.

It is inconceivable that such confusion in lesson materials could have existed so long had it not been for the memoriter method of instruction so universally used. If words are simply to be memorized, then the Bible verses and catechisms without interpretative helps will answer the purpose; but if the material is to be tested by the use which the pupil can make of it immediately, if the arousing in the mind of the pupil of a motive for the study of a particular lesson and an eager desire to know its contents is considered to be the first step in good teaching, then, of course, the curriculum material must be selected and organized with a great deal more care. The middle of the nineteenth century found the Sunday-school world with a growing desire to know the Bible itself. Catechetical interpretations of the Bible or substitutes for Bible study were becoming unpopular, and various publishing agencies, denominational and otherwise, were earnestly seeking to work out the best possible system of lessons out of the Bible itself.

Steps toward graded instruction.—While the curriculum developments which we have just noted were far from satisfactory, they indicate that many people were at work trying to find a better way. They indicate also that considerable effort was being made to work out a graded system of lessons. As we noted in Chapter II, some schools had at an early date a fairly well graded curriculum, selecting the textbooks which were best adapted to the interests and needs of each class. In 1844, in their address to the General Conference, the bishops of the Methodist Episcopal Church made the following plea for graded instruction:

"Sunday-school instruction may justly be regarded as one of the most effectual auxiliaries which we can employ for the prevention of the destructive influence of error, by preoccupying the infant mind with the germs of scriptural truth. Although it is a matter of rejoicing that a great amount of good has been accomplished by this service, it is believed that much more might be done with a system better adapted to the capacities of the subjects of instruction, and with books suitable to different classes in the several stages of improvement. Classification for many reasons has always been regarded as an important provision in a system of instruction, especially for children. We need not enlarge on its utility, but we are deeply impressed with the necessity and obligation of renewed and persevering effort in extending the operation of the institution so as to embrace tens of thousands of the children of our people who have not been brought under its salutary influence, and of revising and improving the system both with respect to the mode of instruction and the books to be used, so as to afford the best helps and the greatest facility in accomplishing its benevolent designs."[8]

PREPARATION FOR THE INTERNATIONAL UNIFORM LESSONS

The student may find it difficult to understand why, in the face of the very significant experiments in graded lesson materials in the first half of the nineteenth century, the Sunday-school world should have moved away from this course toward a uniform lesson system. Several reasons offer a possible explanation but they do not satisfy the mind. Undoubtedly, the desire for uniformity was a reaction against the chaotic state of lesson materials in the so-called "Babel Series." This chaos was due not so much to the experiments in graded instruction as to the efforts of rival publishers and Sunday-school leaders to find the best way and to win a following for their plans. Nevertheless the result was chaotic.

In the second place, the movement for uniformity was aided by the conception that the Bible was the only textbook for Sunday-school lesson material, another outgrowth of the failure to secure satisfactory Bible study in the preceding period and an outgrowth also of the movement in the Sunday-school world to emphasize conversion apart from the development of Christian character. In the third place, the writer believes that

---

[8] *Journal of the General Conference of the Methodist Episcopal Church,* 1840, 44, 48—1844, p. 170.

the uniform lesson system was brought about because a few men such as B. F. Jacobs and John H. Vincent had conducted valuable experiments along this line, and because of their success with these experiments preferred this plan. Being outstanding leaders with a successful experience behind them, it was possible for them to bring the organized Sunday-school forces into harmony with their plan.

In the fall of 1865 Mr. Vincent proposed to an institute conducted by the Chicago Sunday-School Union the following question, "Is it practicable to introduce a uniform system of lessons into all our schools?" In 1866, as editor of *The Sunday-School Teacher*, he began to prepare such a course, entitled "Two Years With Jesus: A New System of Sunday-School Instruction." Although he resigned from his editorship of *The Sunday-School Teacher*, and removed to New York to take charge of the Sunday School Department of the Methodist Episcopal Church after only four months of service as editor, he continued to prepare the lessons through the year 1866 He was followed as editor by the Rev. H. L. Hammond, later by C. R. Blackall, and then by the Rev. Edward Eggleston, who, as Sampey says, "made *The Teacher* in fact as well as in name, *The National Sunday-School Teacher*."[9]

Dr. Vincent and Dr. Eggleston were soon editing rival series of lessons, each of great merit. The former called his Berean Series, while that of the latter was known as the "National Series." As early as 1867 B. F. Jacobs, an organizing genius in the Sunday-school

---

[9] Sampey—*The International Lesson System*, p. 61.

For vivid description of the steps leading up to adoption of the Uniform Lesson System see Sampey, pp. 60ff., who quotes freely from a monograph on *The Lesson System*, by the Rev. Simeon Gilbert.

world, saw the advantages of the scheme of lessons inaugurated by Dr. Vincent and began to be enthused over the possibility of having the Sunday-school world united in the study of one lesson for the whole school and the same lesson everywhere. To the genius of Dr. Vincent and Dr. Eggleston in showing the possible values in such lessons and to that of Mr. Jacobs as promoter and organizer, the International Lesson System owes its birth. Despite the fact that rival publishers and editors wanted their lessons to be the one uniform series, in 1871 Mr. Jacobs had persuaded Dr. Eggleston and Dr. Vincent to compromise and co-operate to the extent that the three of them on August 9, 1871, agreed upon a uniform series of lessons for the year 1872. Two quarters of these lessons were taken from the National Series, one quarter from the Berean Series and a fourth quarter was selected by the three. These lessons were widely adopted in the United States so that when the National Sunday-School Convention met at Indianapolis April 16–19, 1872, a uniform lesson system had been actually in operation nearly four months.

International Lesson Committee Created.—At the International Sunday-School Convention held in Indianapolis, 1872, the proposal to create one International Lesson Committee was brought forward by Mr. B. F. Jacobs, at 9 A. M., on April 18. We are told that as soon as he had finished speaking, cries of "Vote, vote," from all over the house made it evident that the convention was ready to support the proposition almost unanimously. But the convention leaders were unwilling that so important a step should be taken hastily, and action was deferred until the afternoon session, when the motion was carried by an overwhelming majority, only ten voting in the negative. The following were elected as members of the first International Lesson Committee:

Clergymen:

Rev. John H. Vincent, D.D., New York (Methodist Episcopal).

Rev. John Hall, D.D., New York (Presbyterian).

Rev. Warren Randolph, D.D., Pennsylvania (Baptist).

Rev. Richard Newton, D.D., Pennsylvania (Protestant Episcopal).

Rev. A. L. Chapin, D.D., Wisconsin (Congregationalist).

Laymen:

Professor Philip G. Gillett, LL.D., Illinois (Methodist Episcopal).

George H. Stuart, Pennsylvania (Presbyterian).

B. F. Jacobs, Illinois (Baptist).

Alexander G. Tyng, Illinois (Protestant Episcopal).

Henry P. Haven, Connecticut (Congregational).

Dr. John H. Vincent was named as chairman and Dr. Warren Randolph as secretary. Both of these men continued in office for twenty-four years.

It was far more difficult to evolve a working plan and to secure the cooperation of the denominational publishers than to create this committee, but this had already been worked out in a preliminary way before the convention assembled. Hence, without delay, the committee proceeded to its task of creating lesson outlines and selecting daily home Bible readings and the Golden Texts which should embody the central thought of each lesson. As previously stated, there was unanimous agreement that the lessons should be exclusively biblical. They also agreed that the entire Bible should be covered within a cycle of seven years (later modified to six). But what should be the proportion of Old-Testament material to the New, and what should be the arrangement of material were problems which presented much complexity.

The first cycle of lessons.—The first completed cycle was as follows:

UNIFORM LESSONS[10]

1873
  January–March—Studies in the Old Testament (Genesis).

  April–September—Studies in the New Testament (Matthew).

  October–December—Studies in the Old Testament (Genesis).

1874
  January–March—Studies in the Old Testament (Exodus).

  April–June—Studies in the Old Testament (Exodus, Leviticus, Numbers, Deuteronomy).

  July–December—Studies in the New Testament (Mark).

1875
  January–June—Studies in the Old Testament (Joshua, Judges, 1 Samuel).

  July–December—Studies in the New Testament (John).

1876
  January–March—Studies in the Old Testament (1 and 2 Samuel).

  April–June—Studies in the New Testament (Acts).

  July–September—Studies in the Old Testament (1 and 2 Kings, Chronicles, Proverbs).

  October–December—Studies in the New Testament (Acts).

---

[10] *An Aeroplane View of the International Sunday-School Lessons, 1873–1920 (–23) by Years and by Portions.* Compiled from the Records by Professor Ira M. Price, Secretary of the Lesson Committee.

1877   January–June—Studies about the Kingdom of Israel (1 and 2 Kings, Amos, Hosea, Jonah, Nahum).
July–December—Studies in the Acts.

1878   January–June—Studies about the Kingdom of Judah (2 Chronicles, Jeremiah, Daniel).
July–December—Studies in Luke.

1879   January–March—Studies in the Old Testament (Ezra, Nehemiah, Psalms).
April–June—Studies in the Old Testament (Job, Isaiah, Micah, Joel, Ezekiel, Zechariah, Malachi).
July–December—Studies in the New Testament (Epistles, Hebrews, Revelation).

Between 1872 and 1914 no radical modification of these plans for the uniform lessons was made. The proportion of Old-Testament material to that of the New Testament was modified, and the frequency with which the gospel narrative should appear was never quite settled. In other words, experiments in the arrangement of the material were going on throughout the period, but the general plan was the same.

Significance of the International Uniform Lesson System.—That the inauguration of the International Uniform Lesson Plan was one of the most significant events in Sunday-school history every student will readily recognize. That it marked a great forward step in its day no one will refuse to concede. Whether a system of uniform instead of graded lessons was the best possible forward step will ever be a subject for debate. These new lessons did make possible an era of great Sunday-school progress. For about twenty years they seem to have secured real Bible study, aided undoubtedly by the exciting discussions of biblical subjects between biblical critics, so-called "higher and lower critics" and conservative students who opposed the "critical" methods.

But the thoughtful student must also recognize that after these two decades of enthusiastic support it failed very largely as a means of Bible study. The enthusiasm began to wane, the teacher-training classes dwindled in interest, except the "teachers' meetings" for the study of "next Sunday's lesson." Many a teacher, having no enthusiasm or adequate preparation for the work, used with little variation the dry skeleton questions given in the quarterlies and intended to serve only as guides.

The expositions of the biblical passages were ably presented in Sunday-school quarterlies, in weekly periodicals, and often in the daily press. Down to the present these have been written with great expository skill. The lesson helps have improved in form and method, but the general plan of having one common passage of Scripture for all ages did not prove in the long run to be a satisfactory arrangement of biblical material for real study either for the old or for the young. The result was that progressive educational workers exhibited a growing restlessness and opposition to the plan in the last fifteen years of the nineteenth century.

The Primary Union.—This opposition found concrete expression in several movements. Perhaps the most influential single factor in the early stages of the opposition was the National Primary Union, which was formed in 1884 and changed its name to the International Primary Union in 1887.

Among other projects these women definitely set out

to secure a better selection of lesson material for the younger children. They were loyal to the organized Sunday-school movement and had no intention of leading a revolt, but they were determined to secure a reformation of the plan. After repeated efforts, assisted in March, 1894, by a conference between a group of Sunday-school specialists and the Lesson Committee, they succeeded in securing from the Lesson Committee a list of "Optional Primary Lessons for 1896." The following note was prefixed to the list of lessons: "This list of optional primary lessons is prepared by the International Lesson Committee in response to a request from many primary workers who wish a separate primary course, while the committee still believes in the wisdom of *one uniform lesson for all*."[11] The course was issued in the fall of 1895 by the *Sunday School Times*, but no helps were prepared by denominational publishing houses.

The New Jersey School of Methods.—Another agency which became an effective exponent of graded lessons was the Summer School of Primary Methods founded in 1894 by E. Morris Fergusson. Later this school became known as the New Jersey School of Methods for Sunday-School Workers, held at Asbury Park, New Jersey, and has been rightly characterized by Dr. Sampey, when he says, "It has been an experiment station for advanced Sunday-school workers at which teachers have learned while they were imparting instruction to others."[12] Two significant items will illustrate the influence of this school. In 1896 at this summer school, Mrs. J. Woodbridge Barnes proposed to

---

[11] Sampey—*The International Lesson System*, p. 145.
[12] *Ibid.*, p. 16.

her students the following question, "What do we wish our children to know about the Bible before they are twelve years of age?" Together they worked out on the blackboard an outline which became the basis of the Graded Supplemental Lessons of the Elementary Department of the Sunday School, and which were approved by the International Sunday-School Convention of Denver in 1902. The success of these supplemental lessons proved to be a powerful stimulus to creating a demand for international graded lessons because teachers soon began to ask, "Why can we not make this graded supplemental material (usually taught for ten minutes) the main lesson material?"

It was also at the School of Primary Methods at Asbury Park, July 5–10, 1897, that Miss Margaret Cushman, then a public-school kindergarten teacher, gave her lectures on child study. These so impressed the school that some of the leaders asked her if she could work out a system of kindergarten lessons embodying these principles. As the result of this request, on the closing day of the session Miss Cushman handed to those who had interviewed her the night before the outline of a two years' course for children of the kindergarten age. In November, 1898, the Cushman lessons were printed in *The Messenger*, the paper of the New Jersey State Sunday-School Association, and scores of teachers began using them at the beginning of the new year, 1899. These lessons were later revised, issued in book form by the Fleming H. Revell Company, and proved to be very popular forerunners of the new movement.

Dr. Blakeslee's Lessons.—The most formidable opponent of the uniform lessons in the early stages of the opposition was the Rev. Erastus Blakeslee. Coming into touch in the late eighties with William Rainey

Harper and others who were applying the newly discovered psychological principles of learning to Bible study, he determined to introduce these methods into use of Sunday-school lesson material. Failing to influence favorably the International Lesson Committee, he launched his own series of graded lessons. His lessons were at first all biblical, and while not closely graded, they were for four divisions of pupils. Since he was a skillful promoter, he won many supporters among the pastors, editors, and teachers who preferred the newer educational methods.

A GROWING DEMAND FOR A BETTER CURRICULUM

In the early years of the twentieth century the agitation for better methods in religious education gathered strength rapidly. The principles of Pestalozzi, Froebel, and Herbart had by this time greatly modified methods of public-school education. Education was seen to be the unfolding of natural capacities within the child rather than the cramming of something into his mind. The question was being asked, "What knowledge is most useful for the development of a child's capacities in any given period of his growth?" Curriculum material which had heretofore been used in the public schools largely because of its "disciplinary value" was compelled to give way to material which would be immediately useful as well as disciplinary.

The International Uniform Lessons were not selected in harmony with these newer principles which the public school world had been slowly testing and had finally adopted because of their manifestly superior results. In some Sunday schools experiments in harmony with the newer educational practices had been made for several years. The New Jersey Summer

School, as we have already mentioned, was organized for the purpose of providing a training center for those who desired to study Sunday-school work in the light of the latest approved educational principles. The University of Chicago conducted an experimental "model Sunday school" to try out new curriculum material and methods. Such influential books as *Principles and Ideals of the Modern Sunday School* (Burton–Mathews) grew out of this experiment. The Hartford School of Religious Pedagogy was also an influential center at this time in which were produced *The Bible School Curriculum* (Pease), and the writings of Edward Porter St. John. *The Pedagogical Bible School*, by Samuel Hazlett, lecturer in Hartford Theological Seminary 1901–02, was another significant book.

The newly discovered laws of psychology were applied to the study of the development of the religious life by such writers as Starbuck in his *Psychology of Religion*, and Coe in *The Spiritual Life*, and *The Religion of a Mature Mind*. These books were typical of a growing literature applying scientific knowledge to the field of religious education. In 1903 the Religious Education Association was organized by some of the most influential Christian educators in America, and it at once undertook the task of propagating scientific educational ideals in the work of the church. Through its annual conventions, its bimonthly journal, *Religious Education*, and the investigations which have been conducted under its auspices, much has been done in the way of turning the attention of Christian leaders to the opportunities and needs in the field of religious education.

Leadership of Mrs. J. Woodbridge Barnes.—At this point we find coming prominently into the story a little woman, to whom the Sunday-school world owes a greater debt than it can ever pay. She was a leader so modest and quiet in her manner, yet so farseeing, so tactful, and so patient, that in her quiet way she accomplished what many desired but no one else seemed able to bring about. In the first place, she believed in laying the foundation for a new curriculum by careful study of the needs of the child to be taught, and of the various problems which must be solved partially at least before the right kind of curriculum material could be selected. Hence she organized a group to study these problems and to be ready with a program when the hour of opportunity should come.

She herself was the superintendent of the Elementary Division of the International Sunday-School Association. In August, 1906, she received the permission of the International Executive Committee "to cooperate with the Lesson Committee, the Editorial Association, and Denominational bodies, as well as others, who may be planning graded lessons for the Primary and Junior Departments." Having obtained such permission she organized a Graded Lessons Conference.

Graded Lessons Conference.—The workers invited to join this Conference were chosen because of their own personal fitness for such work, their relations to the denominations, their ability to command the services of prominent educators, their sympathy with the problems involved, their geographical location with reference to the necessary place of meeting—Newark, New Jersey —and their willingness to give their time and to pay their own expenses. Those invited into the Conference at the beginning were: Miss Josephine L. Baldwin, Miss Rose Scott, Rev. E. Morris Fergusson, Rev. M. S. Littlefield, Rev. Pascal Harrower, Miss Marianna C.

Brown, Miss F. W. Danielson, Miss E. D. Paxton, Mr. R. E. Diffendorfer, Miss F. H. Darnell, Miss A. B. Hamlin, Miss Margaret Slattery, Prof. E. P. St. John, Miss Marion Thomas, Mrs. M. G. Kennedy, Miss Martha K. Lawson, Mrs. J. Woodbridge Barnes, Mrs. D. M. Krick, Mrs. Alonzo Pettit.

Later when working on Intermediate and Senior Lessons, B. S. Winchester, Sidney A. Weston, Henry H. Meyer, Arlo Ayres Brown, and others were added.

Relations to the International Lesson Committee. —The limits of this book do not permit a detailed discussion of the activities of this group of workers, but the following letters will give some glimpses of how they worked and what were their relations to the International Lesson Committee prior to 1908:[13]

March 27, 1907.

To the International Lesson Committee:
GENTLEMEN:

As members of the Graded Lessons Conference, now in session, we desire that you may be fully advised of our plans, our work, and our relationship to the International Sunday-School Association; particularly as your cooperation is essential to the complete fulfillment of our purpose.

Our desire is to see the present beginners' course of two years suitably revised, and followed with a three years' primary course and a four years' junior course; the whole constituting nine years of graded-lesson material, to the completion of the average pupil's twelfth year. We desire to secure from the International Convention, as was done in the case of the beginners' lessons, a vote of approval and reference of the matter to you, and

---

[13] The following letters are quoted from a paper prepared by Miss Josephine L. Baldwin on "The History of the Graded Lessons Conference."

either before or after such a vote, as you may deem wise, we desire you to consider the plan of lessons which we hope ere long to be able to submit, and issue them with your approval, with such modifications as to your wisdom may seem needful.

We are all of us strongly on the side of the International unity; we believe in our Sunday schools working together; we recognize the continued necessity for an Ungraded International Course; but we know that a proportion of schools far too large to be longer neglected demands graded material for regular lesson work. We feel that it is vital that this material should come to them from the International Lesson Committee, that it should be such as actual teachers of the classes, and grades concerned can use under present circumstances, that it should conform to truth in child study and represent the best available methods in teaching practice, and that its end and ideal should be the salvation of the pupil and the upbuilding of his character.

In 1902 at Denver, as you recall, the conference of elementary grade teachers petitioned the Convention for a two-year Beginners' Course to be issued by you. Similarly at Toronto in 1905, the representative elementary conference, heartily, and without one dissenting vote, expressed its appreciation of the Beginners' lessons and asked for a Primary Course as soon as the way opened to issue it. The matter again came up at the meeting of the Editorial Association in July, 1906, when our chairman by request of that Association presented a paper showing how not only a primary but also a junior graded course is absolutely essential to the present movement for adapted and effective work in the elementary division of the Sunday school.

We as a Conference, were called together by our Chairman, Mrs. J. W. Barnes, with the approval of the International Executive Committee, on the ground that the demand for graded lessons should be led and not merely yielded to by the International Association. The effort was made to secure as members all the lesson writers, State elementary leaders, and specialists in Sunday school pedagogy within practicable distance from Newark, the chairman's city. Several who were earnestly desired found it impossible to attend. The Conference first met in October, 1906, and meetings have since been held about once a month, each meeting lasting two days. We have worked in two sections, primary and junior. The names of those who have taken active part in all or most of the sessions are appended to this letter.

We have agreed upon the needs and interests of pupils in the grades concerned, and the corresponding truths to be embodied in the lessons selected. The choice and arrangement of these lessons is progressing as rapidly as is consistent with a close following of our ideal. We hope ere long to complete a working outline of at least the first year primary and the first year junior, and then to introduce the lessons thus outlined into a number of selected schools for experimental use, before agreeing on our final draft of the course, either in outline or detail.

We rejoice to observe the many other efforts now being made in this same direction, and believe that God's hand is clearly leading us to better and higher things. We believe, too, that when the right material has been found and arranged in the right order the reasons for it will appear. We respectfully ask your sympathy in our efforts and your cognizance of our existence and our purpose.

With great respect, we are yours,
The Graded Lessons Conference.
MRS. J. W. BARNES, *Chairman.*

To which Dr. Schauffler sent the following reply:

NEW YORK, April 1, 1907.

MY DEAR MRS. BARNES:

Yours of the 30th together with communication to the Lesson Committee of March 29th is at hand. It will be placed before the committee at our meeting in April in Boston, and I presume will also come up before the Joint Committee Meeting in London.

The program that you outline is somewhat surprising, for it involves practically a nine years' course of graded lesson material. I shall be exceedingly interested to see where your workers find material for a nine years' graded course that shall be in any true sense graded material. I cannot myself conceive where such material really graded can be found from Genesis to Revelation. However, it may be that the combined intelligence of skilled workers can produce such a course. The graded lessons that I have seen so far have been graded more in name than in fact as to material. Of course, the Lesson Committee will take no action in this matter until after the Louisville Convention, for we are under instructions from the Denver Convention which we are bound to carry out without material deviation.

With very best wishes,

Yours sincerely,

A. F. SCHAUFFLER.

Assistance of denominational editors.—One of the most influential factors in bringing about a system of international graded lessons was the support of certain denominational editors and publishers. Such editors as John T. McFarland, J. R. Miller, B. S. Winchester, C. R. Blackall, E. B. Chappell, and others, supported by their publishers, brought tremendous pressure to bear upon the Lesson Committee in favor of graded lessons.

Leadership within the International Association.— Although neither the International Lesson Committee nor the International Sunday-School Association through its conventions can be said to have taken the initiative in providing a graded-lesson system for the schools, some of the staff of the international and its auxiliary associations were in this matter pioneers. They were rather solitary figures overwhelmed by a multitude who were satisfied with present conditions, and some of these workers found it necessary to resign because out of sympathy with the majority. At the same time they were loyal enough to the Association to adhere to the policy of trying to influence the International Convention and the International Lesson Committee instead of trying to lead a revolt. Mrs. Barnes kept the Lesson Committee fully informed concerning the progress of the Graded Lessons Conference.

The Boston Conference.—But the whole-hearted support of the Association and its Lesson Committee was assured when on January 2, 1908, in the home of Mr. W. N. Hartshorne, chairman of the Executive Committee of the International Sunday-School Association, an informal conference of Sunday-school workers was held. For two days fifty-four men and women sat in conference and debated the question of graded lessons. The following resolutions were passed unanimously:

(1) That the system of a general lesson for the whole school which has been in successful use for thirty-five years is still the most practicable and effective system for the great majority of the Sunday schools of North America. Because of its past accomplishments, its present usefulness, and its future possibilities, we recommend its continuance and its fullest development.

(2) That the need for a graded system of lessons is expressed by so many Sunday schools and workers that it should be adequately met by the International Sunday-School Association, and that the Lesson Committee should be instructed by the next International Convention, to be held in Louisville, Kentucky, June 18–23,

1908, to continue the preparation of a thoroughly graded course covering the entire range of the Sunday school.

The Lesson Committee unanimously adopted these resolutions as a part of its report to the convention in Louisville, and the International Association assembled in the convention also unanimously adopted them.

Immediately upon receipt of this authorization the Lesson Committee asked for the help of the unofficial "Graded Lessons Council," and together they began to organize into final form the lesson outlines.

Important battles for principles.—The battles fought in committee sessions for the next few years were of the highest significance to religious education. They were intense spiritual and intellectual struggles for the truth as each champion saw it. It is fair to say that the groups involved never did come to agreement as to the purpose of a Sunday school and the aims of the curriculum. As history shows, they came to agreement on some essentials, and where they could not agree each group was Christian enough to allow for differences of conviction by assisting in the preparation of alternate courses.

We have stated that the aim of the Sunday school as expressed by its most influential leaders between 1860 and 1890 was twofold—the conversion of the pupil and the imparting of biblical instruction. Some influential members of the International Lesson Committee hold that view to this day. In the years 1908 to 1914 they were distinctly in the majority and the bulk of opinion in the International Conventions seemed to lean that way. They recognized the importance of other materials for Christian instruction but felt that these should be offered through other organizations, and certainly not on Sunday.

The party represented by the Graded Lessons Conference, a few influential editors, and a small minority of the Lesson Committee held that the securing of conversions was not the supreme task of the Sunday school but only the beginning of its task. The supreme task was that of winning recruits and of training them for definite Christian world-wide service. While they did not share entirely the view of such men as Dewey and Thorndike that education is essentially a process of adjustment to environment, they did share with them the view that any true education is essentially a method of developing lives which will be competent to do their share of the world's work.

Some of this progressive party knew through reading and practice the new theories of public-school education with the emphasis upon knowledge that is of the most use, knowledge which fits the capacities of a growing child and enables him to live completely at any given period of his life. Others took their viewpoint from a very practical angle. They asked themselves: "What are we producing as the result of our present curriculum? Are we producing competent parents, good Sunday-school teachers, and effective Christian workers in other lines? A school system must be measured by its fruits. What are the fruits to be expected from seven or fourteen years of study in a uniform lesson curriculum?"

The answer was not satisfactory. One might reasonably expect as fruitage that the boys and girls would commit their lives to Christ, that they would know about the cardinal Christian virtues such as honesty, purity, unselfishness; that they would also know a few Bible stories, and be able to recite a few verses of Scripture. If their teachers possessed striking personalities and gifts for teaching, this knowledge frequently found expression in habits of honesty and service, but there was no sound educational practice in the system itself to guarantee this result. On every hand people were complaining about how little Christians knew about the activities of the local church, or about its missionary enterprises, and even about the great movements in the Bible itself.

The battle over admitting extra-biblical material. —The real battle at this time was not over whether there should be graded lessons or not, but whether any extra-biblical material should be offered in the lessons themselves. When the outline submitted by the Graded Lessons Conference introduced a few missionary heroes in the Junior lessons it seemed to some as if the ark had been touched by unclean hands. To be sure, not even the conservatives had any objections to missionary illustrations; in fact, a large part of the lesson period might be taken up with a discussion of Adoniram Judson without any objections being raised, but the lesson itself should be called a biblical lesson and based on a biblical passage. The "radicals" suggested that they favored devotional Bible readings for every extra-biblical lesson, but that if at a particular time in the boy's life he should study the career of a missionary hero, the lesson title should indicate the real theme.

When a series of thirteen lessons on "Later Christian Heroes" was submitted, including for study Ignatius, Savonarola, Luther, Wesley, and others, the cry went up, "What new heresy is this which you are bringing in?" The answer was, "We are simply trying to line up the Sunday school with its historical antecedents. The early catechetical schools in the days of the apostles and the generations immediately following studied about heroic Christian lives, and sacred writings which were not strictly in the Bible." When two lessons on Maccabean heroes were introduced to bridge over the gap from the days of Malachi to the time of Christ, a brilliant Sunday-school writer opposed the plan with ridicule by publishing in racy style a suggested series to parallel this. The following was a typical lesson:

Subject: John D. Rockefeller.
Golden Text: "My head with oil thou dost anoint."
Lesson Hymn: "Praise John, from whom oil blessings flow."

The article furnished much humor for the Graded Lessons Conference, but had no ill effects upon the forward movement.

It is doubtful if any extra-biblical material would have been approved had it not been for the vigorous championing of this position by such editors as John T. McFarland, Benjamin S. Winchester, and James R. Miller. These were convinced that the curriculum should offer whatever material is necessary to train the Christian for efficient service. They recognized the Bible as the principal source book for Christian education, and, in fact, asked for but very little extra-biblical material. However, they did insist that the subjects of Temperance, Missions, Church History, Church Forms of Organized Work, and Vocational Opportunities should have a place in the regular lessons instead of being presented as supplemental material.[14]

Pressure from the denominations.—Another factor entered into the controversy. The members of the

[14] The policy of using graded supplemental material with the Uniform Lessons had gained considerable popularity prior to 1910, this supplemental material dealing especially with the memorization of Bible verses, the creed, etc. However, it might include other subjects. See p. 103.

International Lesson Committee were responsible not to the denominations which conducted most of the Sunday schools and prepared the great bulk of the literature, but to an international convention. The denominations as such had no representation either in the convention or in the committee. It looked as if an outside committee would refuse to let the editors have with the approval of the International Sunday-School Association, what the editors believed the people wanted and needed. At several stages in the proceedings the editors leading the movement for graded lessons containing extra-biblical material declared that unless such lessons could be provided with the sanction of the Lesson Committee, they would ignore the Committee and prepare their own lesson outlines.

The result was a compromise. The request for approval of extra-biblical material was granted, but alternate courses containing only biblical material were offered for every course in which the extra-biblical material was sanctioned.

Such denominations as the Presbyterian, U. S. A.; the Baptists, North; the Congregationalists, the Disciples, Methodist Episcopal, and the Methodist Episcopal, South, chose the outlines containing a small number of extra-biblical lessons; the Southern Baptists, and other influential denominations chose the outlines containing only the biblical materials. A strong syndicate was formed by the Presbyterians of the North, the Congregationalists, the Methodist Episcopalians, and the Methodists of the South for the publication of International Graded Lessons. The active management of this syndicate was placed in the hands of Mr. Arthur F. Stevens of the Methodist Book Concern, whose intelligent interest and efficient handling contributed largely to the successful introduction of the series. The Baptists of the North published the Keystone Series of International Graded Lessons based upon the same outlines as those used by the syndicate. In 1910 the first years of the Beginners, Primary, and Junior grades were issued. By 1914 the series was practically complete.

Other graded series.—We have already noted how the Bible Study Union (taken over from Dr. Blakeslee by Charles Scribner's Sons), and the Constructive Series (University of Chicago Press) preceded the International Graded Lessons. It should be said also that the Beacon (Unitarian) Series was also a forerunner. In 1916 the Protestant Episcopal Church developed the Christian Nurture Series along very similar lines to those of the other series, but using the Church Year as the basis of organization. Other denominations printed series following one or another of the International Lesson Committee's outlines.

LATER DEVELOPMENTS

Since 1910 the graded-lesson courses have been growing in popularity. Those containing the extra-biblical material were subjected to intense criticism in the early years; in part because of the extra-biblical lessons, and in part because the biblical lesson treatments were said to set forth liberal views which eliminated the miraculous and other vital elements. The answer was that no vital elements were omitted or slighted. The difficulty lay in expecting to find a full treatment of all points such as an adult would desire in the material prepared for younger pupils. The Presbyterian (U. S. A.) General Assembly in 1913 appointed a Committee of Investigation with power, and this committee compelled their publishers to withdraw from the syndicate. They withdrew and prepared a system of "departmentally graded lessons," which were largely an adaptation of the completely graded outlines. The Presbyterian and Reformed Churches have zealously promoted these, and in the more recent years with considerable success.

The great majority of Sunday-school leaders have for several years been vigorous promoters of some form of graded lessons, and the series as it existed in 1915 remains substantially as it was then with respect to topics although many of the textbooks have had one revision.

The Lesson Committee reorganized.—In 1914 the International Lesson Committee was reorganized, so that its membership should be composed as follows:

(1) Eight members elected by the International Sunday-School Association.

(2) Eight members elected by the Sunday-School Council of Evangelical Denominations.

(3) One member selected by each denomination represented in the Sunday-School Council, and having a lesson committee.

When the denominational and Sunday-School Council members took their seats many of them had been instructed to stand for just two types of lesson series:

(1) A completely graded-lesson series.

(2) A departmentally graded-lesson series.

This would abolish the International Uniform Series which had been unchanged by the agitation for graded lessons, and which still commanded a large following. While the friends of a Uniform Lesson Series were probably in a minority in the new Lesson Committee, the other members, for the sake of harmony, consented to delay pushing their proposition. They did, however, modify somewhat the Uniform Lesson Series so that the principle of uniformity was maintained through a common Golden Text, common Daily Bible Readings, and, so far as possible, a common portion of the Scriptures for the lesson material. This section of the Scriptures, however, might include several chapters instead of just one short passage. Separate lesson topics were selected for four age-groups, Primary, Junior, Intermediate-Senior, and Young People-Adult. If necessary, separate portions of Scripture were chosen, but the common general theme remained unless it was obviously unsuited to the younger children. This resulted frequently in a separate lesson for the youngest children, but the lessons for the older groups were not greatly modified.

For several years following 1914 the subcommittee on Uniform Lessons and the subcommittee on Graded Lessons in the International Lesson Committee, worked diligently to perfect their series. A special committee on Adult Courses prepared several outlines for special adult courses—mostly biblical but not exclusively so. The subcommittee on Departmentally Graded Lessons kept on the alert waiting for an opportunity to secure a favorable hearing. In April, 1920, the Graded Lesson Committee presented a report asking for a careful new investigation of the entire field of curriculum needs. At the same time the Committee on Departmentally Graded Lessons pleaded for prompt action. In fact, a definite scheme for Primary departmental lessons was being presented at this session through the initiative of a member of the Uniform Lesson Committee who saw that the Primary adaptation of the Uniform Lesson was a handicap to the improvement and success of a "Uniform Lesson Series."

Revisions in prospect.—It was generally felt to be inexpedient to launch three lesson systems, namely, a closely graded, a departmentally graded, and a uniform, so a committee of seven, under the chairmanship of Luther A. Weigle, was appointed to survey the whole field. The gist of the report of his committee as adopted in December, 1920, is as follows:

In the first place, the commission indicated the scope of its investigations. Questionnaires had been sent to six hundred and twenty-seven carefully selected persons from the following groups: (a) editors of the various publishing houses, denominational and commercial; (b) general, district, and local Sunday-school workers as well as other experts in religious education; (c) heads of departments of religious education in various universities and theological seminaries which maintain, in one form or another, experimental schools of religion. While only one hundred and eighty-seven replies were received, they were so widely distributed geographically and denominationally as to warrant very significant conclusions. The commission reported that the tabulation and evaluation of the various materials "made clear the following facts":[15]

Results of investigation.—

1. There is general commendation of such improvement of the Uniform Lessons as has been secured by their departmental adaptation. The figures submitted to the Commission indicate that the use of the Uniform and Improved Uniform Lessons, though growing in some

---

[15] Quoted from report of the Commission as submitted to the International Lesson Committee. For complete report of actions taken by the Committee at its meetings in Atlantic City, Dec. 29, 30, 1920, see "The International Sunday-School Lesson Committee, Dec., 1917–Sept., 1921. Reports, Actions and Output, Part 2," by Professor Ira M. Price, Secretary of the Lesson Committee, Chicago, 1922.

denominations, is on the whole not keeping pace with the growing enrollment of the Sunday schools.

2. The International Graded Lessons are rapidly growing in circulation and are giving general satisfaction both in their original closely graded form, and as departmentally adapted.

3. There is a widespread demand for courses graded by age groups.

4. Certain additional needs are emphasized by the returns as not being adequately met by existing lesson systems. These include (a) Material suited to stimulate a personal decision for Christ and commitment to his service through membership in the church. (b) Material designed to train the pupil in the functions and duties of church membership. (c) Material suited to stimulate and guide a religious choice of a lifework. (d) Material suitable for training in worship. (e) Material, well chosen and properly ordered, for memorization. (f) Material for missionary education.

5. Our correspondents in general agree that a system of lessons for the Sunday school should be pupil-centered rather than material-centered. The aim of the curriculum should be to nurture the growing moral and religious life of the child, and to lead to a permanent commitment of that life to God through Jesus Christ, and to fitness for service in his kingdom. The lesson materials should be chosen with a view to their fitness to accomplish this aim throughout the varying periods of the child's growth, rather than with a view to their logical completeness or chronological order.

6. Many of our correspondents voice the conviction that neither the Uniform Lessons nor the Graded Lessons impart a complete enough knowledge of the Bible, or give to the pupil the disposition and the ability to use God's Word intelligently. At the same time the need is expressed for enough extra-biblical material from nature and present-day social life to give to the pupil a religious

attitude toward the world in which he lives, and for enough extra-biblical historical material to give the pupil an adequate impression of the continuity of God's presence and purpose in history.

7. The curriculum should give more opportunity for pupil activity, for training in Christian service, and for the motivation of instruction by the problems and purposes of the pupil in connection with this activity, as well as for the expression in this activity of ideas imparted in instruction.

8. There is a growing demand and opportunity for week-day religious instruction. It would be unfortunate to have a week-day curriculum of religion constructed independently of the curriculum of the Sunday school.

9. The whole of our correspondence has deepened our sense of the value of the interdenominational cooperation in which the churches have now engaged for nearly fifty years through the International Sunday-School Lesson Committee. This is a thing to be safeguarded and strengthened.

10. There is a widespread demand for simplicity, stability, and definiteness in the procedure and policy of this Committee.

Recommendations

Your Commission recommends:

1. That we construct all of our lessons hereafter upon the principle of gradation, recognizing two basic types of Sunday-school lesson:

(a) Lessons graded by years.

(b) Lessons graded by age-groups.

2. That the present system of International Graded Lessons be not now further revised by this Committee, the denominations being free as heretofore to make such revision as they may choose.

3. That the Committee proceed with the construction of a system of lessons graded to meet the needs of each of five age-groups:

(a) Primary: ages 6, 7, 8; Grades 1, 2, 3.
(b) Junior   "   9, 10, 11   "   4, 5, 6.
(c) Intermediate " 12, 13, 14   "   7, 8, 9.
(d) Senior   " 15, 16, 17   "   10, 11, 12.
(e) Adult (including young people).

That these lessons be predominantly biblical in contents, consecutive and cumulative, and that they aim to impart a comprehensive knowledge of the Bible, and that they give to the pupil the ability and disposition to use the Word of God intelligently; that they be dated, and that they move in a three-year cycle for each group.

4. That as an integral part of this system of lessons the Committee provide a dated series of services of worship with correlated materials for memorization, for the use of the whole school or of such departments as may desire it, together with materials for Daily Bible Readings and Family Worship.

5. That the new system of lessons thus to be constructed be known officially as The International Sunday-School Lessons: Group Graded Series, and that the present system of graded lessons which is to continue without revision by the Committee be known officially as The International Sunday-School Lessons: Closely Graded Series. That we recognize as short popular titles for these two systems the following:

(a) International Group Lessons.
(b) International Graded Lessons.

6. That the new system of International Group Lessons shall replace the Improved Uniform Lessons beginning January 1, 1924. . . . (Amended.)

A seventh recommendation was adopted as follows: "That the International Sunday-School Lesson Committee proceed, as rapidly as may be possible, with the construction of a new curriculum of religious education which shall provide in integrated fashion for both Sunday and week-day hours, this to be known as 'The International Curriculum of Religious Education.'"

Except for eliminating the date when the International Group Lessons should replace the Improved Uniform Lessons, only minor amendments were offered to the report of the commission. The large representative company of workers present at this session of the committee felt that a very valuable analysis of the situation had been made. However, after debate, it was the unanimous desire of the committee to withhold judgment concerning the extent to which the Group Graded Lessons should replace the Improved Uniform Lessons until the Commission should submit the actual new series of lesson titles. The Commission submitted lesson titles and readings for the Primary and Junior groups, three years each, at the meeting of the Lesson Committee in September, 1921, and the material was released for general criticism. Final action approving these lessons was taken in April, 1922, and the action with reference to substitution of these for the Improved Uniform was as follows: "Resolved, That in view of the exceptional character of the Improved Uniform Lessons for 1924, and in view of the fact that adaptations of these lessons to the Primary and Junior grades have already been made by the Sub-committee on Improved Uniform Lessons, the Secretary be authorized to issue, as a supplement to the Improved Uniform Lessons for 1924, for the information and assistance of publishers and denominational lesson committees, the adaptations already made." According to this action Sunday-school editors and publishers may offer to their people for the year 1924 with the sanction of the Lesson Committee: (a) International Graded Lessons; (b) International Group

Lessons for the Primary and Junior groups, with International Improved Uniform Lessons for the Intermediate-Senior, Young People-Adult groups; (c) International Improved Uniform Lessons for all four age-groups.

SUMMARY

We have devoted this entire chapter to tracing the development of the curriculum that has been most widely used by the leading Protestant denominations. An adequate presentation of the subject would call for a careful analysis of the curricula of the Roman Catholic, the Jewish, the Mormon, the Christian Science, and other Sunday schools, together with curricula for week-day schools, but the limits of this chapter do not permit such treatment.

We have traced the development of curricula in religious education from the *Hornbook* and *New England Primer* of the public-school colonial days down to the closely graded series of Sunday-school lessons of the present period. Other curricula developments are under way, but to these we will give attention in another chapter. In general, the development of curricula in the Sunday school has paralleled that of the public school. It has not taken in so wide a range of materials but it has gradually increased the range of its subjects, and it has come to test all of this material by the question, "Is it useful to prepare the pupil for his place in the social process?" which to the Christian means his place in bringing about the kingdom of God on earth.

Much remains to be done to perfect the selection and organization of material, but where used by competent teachers it is actually producing competent Christian fathers and mothers, teachers and other workers. In the minds of many progressive leaders all of the present series or systems of graded lessons place too much emphasis upon imparting information either biblical or extra-biblical and give too little attention to the lessons that are to be learned in the pupil's immediate environment.[16] They would have the curricula organized so that the approach would be made through the problems arising out of the pupil's environment. The future curricula will doubtless place more emphasis upon the student's immediate interests and problems, but will not neglect to equip him with the knowledge of the essential religious and social facts which he needs as preparation for Christian service.

Topics for discussion:

1. Why does a curriculum refuse to "stay put"? Is there any danger of making a pupil the slave to a curriculum which does not fit his needs? If so, what remedies do you recommend?
2. Try to estimate what type of religious character the curriculum of the colonial period would produce.
3. Try to estimate what type of religious character the day school curriculum of 1800–1840 would produce; also what type the Sunday-school curriculum of the same period would produce.
4. Make the same estimate for the period 1870 to 1890.
5. Would you have voted for an International Uniform Lesson System if you had been at the Indianapolis Convention in 1872? Explain how you would have voted, and why.

---

[16] George Albert Coe—*Opposing Theories of the Curriculum.* Religious Education, April, 1922, p. 43ff.

6. In view of the fact that there were many experiments with some form of graded lessons prior to 1860, how do you account for the overwhelming, almost unanimous, vote in the convention in Indianapolis for Uniform Lessons?

7. Has the influence of denominational publishing houses in curriculum matters been on the whole good or bad?

8. From the standpoint of the needs of pupils in 1908, what were the merits and defects of the International Uniform Lesson System?

9. Which do you favor for a Sunday school of three hundred pupils in a community of average intelligence: a closely graded system of lessons for the entire school, or a uniform lesson for all pupils above eleven years of age? What are some of the tests which a curriculum for a particular Sunday school should meet?

10. Compare some of the principal series of textbooks used in Sunday schools of to-day.

11. What should be the next step in curriculum making?

Brief bibliography of selected references:

Sampey—*The International Lesson System.* The Sunday-School Board of the Southern Baptist Convention and Fleming H. Revell Company, New York, 1911.

Cubberley—*Public Education in the United States.* Houghton Mifflin Company, Boston, 1919.

Rice—*Important and Remarkable Epochs in the History of Sunday Schools.* American Sunday-School Union, 1905.

Pease—*An Outline of a Bible School Curriculum.* The University of Chicago Press, Chicago, 1904.

Burton–Mathews—*Principles and Ideals for the Mod-*

ern Sunday School. The University of Chicago Press, Chicago, 1903.

Hazlett—*The Pedagogical Bible School.* Fleming H. Revell Company, New York, 1903.

Coe—*Education in Religion and Morals.* Fleming H. Revell Company, New York, 1904.

Forbush—*The Coming Generation.* D. Appleton and Company, New York, 1912.

Meyer—*The Graded Sunday School in Principle and Practice.* Eaton & Mains, New York, 1910.

Athearn—*The Church School.* The Pilgrim Press, Boston, 1914.

Leaflets prepared by the publishers of Sunday-school lesson materials, by denominational Sunday-school Boards, and by the International and State Sunday-School Associations or Councils.

CHAPTER VI

THE EVOLUTION OF THE TEACHER-TRAINING MOVEMENT

No school system can rise higher than the ability of its teachers. We are not surprised that American public schools made so little progress for a hundred and fifty years when one teacher worked every lesson out with each individual pupil instead of conducting class recitations. Nor could we expect a great deal more except improved memorization, and perhaps improved writing from the Lancastrian monitor system, where the school was divided into groups of ten under a captain who knew little more than the pupils, but who had a drill schedule before him and therefore could speed up the progress of a pupil in some forms of development. Probably even the poorest Sunday-school teacher of that day was quite as competent to instruct as these youthful monitors were—the difference however being that the monitors did have material better suited to their purpose than many of the Sunday-school teachers had.

EARLY STAGES OF DEVELOPMENT

The Sunday-school teaching force of America has been developed upon a volunteer basis—whether rightly or wrongly some one else must say. However, the student of history will probably admit that no scheme ever devised outside of the family has secured so much free time placed at the disposal of children for their guidance as the Sunday school with its volunteer teachers. The plan has serious defects as well as great merits, but it made a nation-wide system of religious schools possible.

It would look to the writer as if the ability of the average Sunday-school teacher for the first forty years of the last century was not far below that of the average public-school teacher. Separate classrooms for the grades did not come into common use in the public schools until about 1840. The public-school teacher had some advantage in the improving lesson materials while the Sunday-school teacher was drilling his pupils in the memorizing of catechisms and Bible verses. However, the advantage of time has always been with the public-school teacher, for one day out of the week is not enough for religious instruction, and the usual one hour allotted out of this day is altogether inadequate.

Rise of the State normal school.—But the greatest difference between public-school teachers and Sunday-school teachers came when the normal schools, in the face of much opposition, rapidly vindicated themselves and the normal-school movement became popular. How slow this movement was in getting under headway in the United States is shown by the following table:[1]

The States which established normal schools before 1860 and their order of establishment were:

```
1839 Massachusetts (1st)
1839      "        (2nd)
1840      "        (3rd)
1844 New York
1849 Connecticut
1849 Michigan
1854 Massachusetts (4th)
```

---

[1] Cubberley—*Public Education in the United States*, p. 293. Houghton Mifflin Company, publishers. Used by permission.

1854 Rhode Island
1855 New Jersey
1857 Illinois
1859 Pennsylvania
1860 Minnesota

But after the success of the normal school at Elmira, New York, and of others, improvements in public-school work came rapidly. It is significant that the completion of the separation between church schools and State schools paralleled these years when the normal schools were getting under headway. Ignorance of teaching methods and sectarian rivalry both held back the public-school progress, but after the Civil War, as we have noted, the improvement of the public schools was rapid.

Early appeals for training of Sunday-school teachers.—Before considering the program of teacher training, let us consider again what was the aim of the Sunday school of the first half of the eighteenth century. The primary aim was clearly "conversion" rather than Christian nurture. The nurture processes were drills in reciting the catechism and Bible verses. That some workers had a better conception of how to teach religion is clearly shown by such books of the time as, *The End and Essence of Sabbath School Teaching*, mentioned in the preceding chapter. Horace Bushnell's *Christian Nurture* was prophetic of a distant new day, also the appeal of the Methodist bishops for graded lessons in 1844. Everyone probably knew even in that remote day that the memorizing of catechisms and Bible verses was not sufficient to guarantee growth into strong Christian character, but the majority of the leaders clearly limited the Sunday school to this phase of Christian nurture.

The Rev. D. P. Kidder, D.D., in 1847, then corresponding secretary of the Sunday-School Union of the Methodist Episcopal Church, in his annual report made the following plea in behalf of normal Sunday schools:

In addition to the means hitherto employed to advance this cause, we think it time to ask whether a system of normal Sabbath-school instruction may not be established. Schools thus designated have been founded by several States of this republic, for the express purpose of training and qualifying teachers for common schools.

Besides the regular institutions founded and supported by the States, voluntary organizations called "Teachers' Institutes," have been formed, with a kindred object, in many of the counties, especially of the State of New York. At these institutes, which are only of brief duration, the time is devoted to mutual improvement by means of lectures, reviews, examinations in different branches of study, and explanations of different modes of teaching and governing. Such meetings of teachers, if judiciously conducted, can hardly fail to be profitable; and they give occasion to ask why Sunday-school teachers may not have similar means of improvement? Perhaps a basis for them is already established in our district Sunday-school conventions, and in the courses of lectures often delivered to Sunday-school teachers.

Why may not these be rendered more practical, and consequently more interesting? Even if *all* the teachers of a district could not meet during a sufficient length of time to take a complete series of lessons on the best methods of Sunday-school instruction, those who could, if representatives of the different schools, might return and impart the knowledge they had received to their several associates. In cities, if the spirit of the enterprise sufficiently prevailed, normal classes of Sunday-school teachers might be organized whenever the services of a competent person could be secured to conduct them. Who can tell what an amount of good might be accomplished were some dozens of our most successful and competent laborers in our Sunday schools to devote a portion of their time, annually, to training teachers on the plan now suggested? Could they succeed, by such means, in elevating the general character of Sunday-school instruction? Could they give a new impetus to one of the greatest benevolent movements of the age? Could they, by moving upon the minds of some hundreds of teachers, influence the hearts and character of thousands of children? Would they regret any sacrifices necessary to accomplish such glorious ends?[2]

The following year he again referred to the subject as follows:

"The proposal of normal instruction for Sabbath-school teachers was suggested in our last report. We confess, however, that we fear the day is distant when the church will take as high ground on this subject as that assumed by several States of the Union, viz., that in order to promote general education most effectually institutions must be provided for the special instruction of teachers."[3]

Early normal courses.—Although Dr. Kidder was apparently discouraged over the slow progress being made in normal instruction for Sunday-school teachers, it must not be thought that nothing was being done in this direction. A few schools under competent leadership were providing programs for the training of their teachers. The following is taken from the frontispiece of one of the earliest teacher-training textbooks:

---

[2] *Annual Report of the Sunday-School Union of the Methodist Episcopal Church*, published by Lane & Tippett, New York, 1847, pp. 47, 48.

[3] See report of 1848, p. 99.

The
Teacher Taught:
An
Humble Attempt
to Make the
Path of the Sunday School Teacher
Straight and Plain.
Written for the American Sunday-School Union and Revised
By the Committee of Publication
Philadelphia
(1839).

This book contains nineteen chapters and three hundred ninety-five pages. A few of the chapter headings are as follows: "On the Origin and Progress of Sunday Schools," "On the Organization of Sunday Schools," "On the Superintendent," "On the Personal Duties and Qualifications of Sunday School Teachers," "On Teachers' Meetings," "On the Susceptibility of Children to Religious Impressions."

The following quotation is significant: "When we speak of religious education we mean, of course, education for God, and this implies (as we have already hinted) not merely education in the science of religion, but the feeling and experience of its transforming power upon the heart. . . . We mean that the grand ultimate object of all his tutors and governors in every branch and department of instruction will be, with God's blessing, to make him while he is a child a believer in the Bible, and (so far as religion is concerned) nothing but the Bible."[4]

The success of the State normal schools seems to have had an immediate effect upon Sunday-school leaders. In 1860 Dr. John H. Vincent, speaking to his ministerial colleagues in Galena, Illinois, asked, "Why can we not have a teachers' institute, similar

---

[4] *The Teacher Taught*, pp. 370, 371. The American Sunday-School Union, publishers. Used by permission.

to that of the public schools, in every district?" And they answered, "We will." In 1862 he said in the London Convention: "We cannot have normal colleges yet in every community, so I recommend that we do the best we can with opportunities now within our reach. In training teachers we must first secure a profound personal conviction of the responsibilities of the teacher's office in the mind of the young candidate. Once make him feel that and he will learn. Without that conviction no combination of circumstances, no outward appliances, can make a teacher of him. Having this, then give him books to read on the subject. I recommend Mr. Inglis' book on *The Sabbath School*, having used it in American Sunday School Normal Classes as a textbook for two years."[5] After speaking of organizing normal classes and conducting weekly teachers' meetings, he remarks, "If we cannot have perfect normal colleges, let us use all the little common appliances we have."[6]

"The Sunday-School Teachers' Institute."— Another glimpse of the teacher-training movement may be caught from the words of John S. Hart in the introduction to the book entitled *The Sunday-School Teachers' Institute*, published in 1866:

It is time that some general movement was made in the matter of teacher training. Of the three hundred thousand teachers who are guiding and sustaining the great work of instruction probably less than one tenth have ever had any regular professional training for the business of teaching. . . .

Why should not our theological seminaries make some provision on this subject? A young man goes to a

[5] Report of Convention, p. 153.
[6] *Ibid.*, p. 153.

theological seminary for the purpose of being fitted and trained for the pastoral office. In the providence of God, and the practical working of Christian institutions at this time, a large portion of the pastor's work—that part of his work too which is most productive of results—lies among the young of his flock.

Let the plain, painful truth be spoken. Our Sabbath schools are taught by those who know not how to teach. Of course there are many brilliant exceptions. I speak only of the general fact. Yet these unskilled teachers, with all their imperfections as teachers, are among the noblest Christians in the land. No one knows so well as they themselves do the extent of their deficiencies and imperfections. No one longs as they do for the knowledge and the skill to do better. Their hearts ache for the longing they have to serve the Master efficiently in this glorious cause. There is no fear that they will not respond to any well-considered and practical plan by which their talents may be guided and their laborious services made more effectual. What the leaders in Israel, the wise men in the church, the ministers and superintendents, the working and thinking men of large hearts and long heads owe to this cause, is the devising and maturing of plans for the improvement of our Sabbath-school teachers. Our schools will never accomplish what they should do until our teachers know better how to teach and what to teach. Our teachers must themselves be taught. Whoever shall devise the means of doing this effectually will help forward the great cause as much as if they were to put a hundred missionaries in the field.[7]

According to Dr. Vincent: "The chief aim of the Sunday school is the spiritual culture of its members. It should bring children to Jesus, and train them for his service."[8] How well Dr. Vincent's plans for teacher

---

[7] J. H. Vincent—*The Sunday-School Teachers' Institute*. Adams Blackmer and Lyon, Chicago, 1866.

[8] *Ibid.*, p. 7.

training were matured by the year 1866 is shown by the following outline of his aims and of the course:

1. The success of teachers' institutes in advancing the interests of secular education throughout the country, has suggested to some earnest friends of the Sunday school the practicability and desirableness of adopting a similar method for the promotion of the higher and nobler ends which this institution contemplates. In these institutes methods of teaching are announced and illustrated. Experienced educators unfold the underlying principles of training. The comparison of plans excites animated discussion. Suggestions are made which quicken and strengthen all who hear them. Youthful teachers go to their work with new purposes and plans for personal culture and professional labor. The institute exercises make a constant demand for intellectual effort. Thus they are a means of mental discipline.

2. In addition to these elements of the institute one other is needed in its adaptation to the Sunday-school system—a Sunday-school teachers' curriculum. We need a regular course of preparatory study, which all enterprising teachers, and candidates from our senior classes for the teacher's office, may pursue.

3. We offer the following, as a general course of study, to meet this demand. Let it comprise:

A series of about fifty exercises, to extend through one or two years, as circumstances may determine, as follows:

(1) Five lectures by a professional and experienced teacher, on the principles and art of teaching.

(2) Ten lectures on the Bible, its history, writers, inspiration, original languages, style, evidences, etc., with lectures on biblical criticism.

(3) Ten specimen lessons for infant, advanced, and adult classes.

(4) Ten exegetical exercises, from the Old- and New-

Testament history, from the Psalms, Prophecies, and Epistles.

(5) Ten catechetical lessons for concert recitation on Bible history, geography, chronology, ancient manners and customs, etc., covering in comprehensive lessons the field of biblical archæology.

(6) Five lectures on the organization, objects, history, management, church relations, and development of the Sunday-school work.[9]

Then he recommends reading exercises by pastors, theological seminaries, higher institutes, especially our female seminaries, local unions, and summer institutes of "three to four weeks," taking candidates through the course in this time.

The work of R. G. Pardee.—Mention should also be made of the institute work in New York conducted in "the fifties" and "sixties" by R. G. Pardee, a layman who gave himself devotedly and with great effectiveness to the improvement of Sunday-school teaching. His work, *The Sabbath School Index,*[10] 1869, was a very useful textbook heartily recommended by Dr. Vincent. He also wrote a little manual, published in 1853, entitled *The Sunday School Worker Assisted.*[11]

Slow progress up to 1866.—Notwithstanding the worthy efforts to train teachers which we have noted prior to 1866 the progress was slow. Teacher-training developments in the public-school world were just beginning to make headway, and they were very much slower in the field of religious education. Despite the earnestness and devotion of the teachers to the cause of Bible study the period was not one of successful Bible study. Pupils memorized many Bible verses, but they

[9] J. H. Vincent—The Sunday-School Teachers' Institute, p. 12.
[10] Published by J. C. Garrigues & Co., Philadelphia.
[11] Published by the New York Sunday-School Union, 1853.

were not taught how to use these verses, nor what relation these messages sustained to great movements in Bible history which gave Christianity to the world.

The awakening.—The next generation of Sunday-school leaders determined to raise up a company that knew the Bible, its geography, its history, and its doctrinal messages as well as many helpful verses. John H. Vincent himself had a passion for biblical geography, having as a pastor formed "Palestine Clubs" in his own churches and elsewhere. To fix the facts in one's memory some of the lessons were put to music. The students memorized by singing just as pupils in the public schools were memorizing some of their political geography lessons by putting the facts to rime and music. Museums with objects from Bible lands were recommended. Traveling museums were not uncommon, and churches which could develop such for themselves were encouraged to do so. A great relief map of Jerusalem and its environs, now standing under a permanent roof in Ocean Grove, is a relic of this enthusiasm. Chautauqua has another one of those maps which is even more famous. The forerunner of these was a relief map on the lawn of Dr. Vincent's church when he was pastor at Camptown, now Irvington, New Jersey.

For some reason the enthusiasm for biblical geography did not last as long as one might expect—perhaps because only a really good biblical student can make the subject thrilling. The teacher-training textbooks for 1875 to 1910 give large place to it, but nevertheless the subject did not maintain its popularity as other phases of Bible study did. The study of biblical passages for expository use was an outstanding passion of this period. Clearly, between the years 1873 and 1890 the program of Bible study recommended by the International Lessons was immensely popular.

That the leaders of this period were also successful in winning converts the work of Dwight L. Moody, an ardent Sunday-school man, clearly shows. But this period emphasized conversion and a particular program of Bible study rather than conversion and nurture in Christian faith and practice. The Bible study was clearly a great advance over the study of catechism and Bible in the preceding period, but the ideals were not defined sharply enough and the curriculum was not broad enough to equip a student for the skillful performance of his Christian duties.

AN ERA OF GREAT ADVANCE

The first twenty years after the Civil War mark one of the greatest eras of progress in Sunday-school history. We have already noted the inauguration of the International Uniform Sunday-School Lessons in 1873 which so wise and careful a student of Sunday-school progress as Jesse Lyman Hurlbut has declared personally to the writer to be "the greatest single step ever taken by the Sunday school." He affirmed further, in reply to a question, that there was no doubt but that this significant step was made possible by the rising popular interest in teacher training. It was a great constructive period. The people were aroused to feel the importance of religious education for young and old as never before, and in the light of public-school experience they knew that trained teachers were a necessity. John H. Vincent, who had been taken out of the pastorate and had been selected as a secretary for Sunday-school promotion by his denomination, organized a "normal college" in 1867. John F. Goucher, later president of Goucher College, received the first diploma awarded for the completion of this course.

In brief, the course covered the following subjects: I. The Bible. II. Interpretation of the Bible. III. Contents of the Bible. IV. How to Teach the Bible. In the beginning outlines were prepared upon the lessons and required readings assigned, but no textbooks were written and the churches were expected to secure lecturers who were competent to present the material required by the outlines. So difficult was it for classes to arrange for these required lectures that Dr. Vincent sought for a place where those who had read the prescribed books could assemble to receive the prescribed lectures and planned for a summer assembly where they could be given. Thus the origin of the assembly at Lake Chautauqua in 1874.

That the movement was spreading through the leading denominations is shown by the following preface in the *Normal Class Manual*, published by The Bible and Education Society of Philadelphia. The Introduction says: "This book is an outgrowth of the National Baptist Sunday-School Convention held in Cincinnati, November, 1872. It is designed to meet a long-felt want to which the Convention gave its most earnest attention."[12] The Preface also contains the following statement by outstanding leaders of several denominations:

In view of the widespread and growing interest in the training of Sunday-school teachers, the undersigned Christian workers, who have given the subject special study and acquired experience in its methods, unite in recommending the formation of normal classes, in connection with the Sunday schools and seminaries of learn-

---

[12] *Normal Class Manual*, p. 4. The Bible and Education Society, Philadelphia. Used by permission.

ing for the benefit of those who would become proficient Bible teachers.

We also agree in recommending the main features of the subjoined outline of elementary study, with the understanding that such modifications may be made in our respective Manuals as will not destroy the essential unity of the plan.

WARREN RANDOLF.   J. H. VINCENT.
H. CLAY TRUMBULL.   J. BENNETT TYLER.[13]

The Chautauqua movement.—The Chautauqua movement[14] began as a means for the training of Sunday-school teachers. If it could have remained permanently such an instrument, the cause of religious education would be much farther advanced to-day, nearly fifty years after the launching of the movement, than it is. The "Assembly" at Lake Chautauqua, New York, was started in 1874 by Dr. Vincent and Lewis Miller, a Sunday-school superintendent, primarily for the purpose of enabling students who were unable to hear the required lectures in their home communities to make up these requirements for the diploma of the normal college. For the first three years it confined itself largely to this purpose, but soon the program was broadened to include general culture, and Chautauqua became a kind of "university of the people." Dr. Vincent and his colleagues organized the Chautauqua Literary and Scientific Circle in 1878. Textbooks not only on Bible study but on many phases of culture were prepared for popular reading and study. The idea was to bring to all classes of people, in simple, condensed form, knowledge of the most important culture of the past and present.

[13] *Normal Class Manual*, p. 4.
[14] Hurlbut—*The Story of Chautauqua*, p. 28. G. P. Putnam's Sons, New York, 1921. Used by permission.

Little Chautauquas sprang into being all over the country. Reading circles to study the course in the home community became popular. The movement has been a blessing to thousands, and if the cause of teacher training suffered as a consequence of the broader program, no one will blame the leaders who achieved such beneficent results through increasing the culture of multitudes. But the fact remains that while teacher-training courses have always been given during the sessions of the parent Chautauqua, this assembly gave up its chief significance to the Sunday-school movement when it undertook the broader program. Perhaps the result would have been different if John H. Vincent had not been made bishop in the Methodist Episcopal Church, thereby coming into duties which necessarily took him out of the teacher-training field. But the fact remains that a great enterprise originally inaugurated for the training of Sunday-school teachers developed into an institution of great power and benefit to the world along other lines, and in adopting its broader program ceased to lead the movement for training teachers of religion.

Success and failure.—The historians must record a popular enthusiasm for teacher training between the years 1867 and 1890. The articles published in this period indicate that many felt themselves to be at the beginning of a great new day in religious education. But the historian must also record that the new day which seemed to be dawning did not really come. As we shall see in a later chapter, Dr. Vincent expected the Christian colleges at once to establish chairs for the training of teachers of religion, but the chairs were not established to any great extent for many years. He expected training classes in the local church to become universal. Instead, many were established and the movement flourished for a few years only to die down and to degenerate too often into a form of "teachers' meetings" for the study of next Sunday's International Uniform Lesson.

Causes of failure.—Such a revival of interest in teaching could not fail to make a permanent contribution to civilization, and the world is greatly indebted to those who launched so ambitious an enterprise and who kept it going long enough to show its possibilities. The movement was not only handicapped by loss of consecutive leadership and by a dissipation of attention, but also because the educational ideals of these leaders were not adequate. They shared the popular ideals of their day and worked with the tools and curricula elements which had popular approval. Culture for the sake of producing a well-informed, high-minded individual was the goal of general education from the primary school to the college in those days. The only cultural material which seemed to be the church's responsibility was found in the Bible. The unity of the educational process was not then widely recognized. Psychology was called "mental science," and in its modern form was scarcely known until near the close of the last century. Educators really thought that great quantities of information could be crammed into a young mind and then be drawn out years later "on demand" whenever the emergency should arise. And if by chance these "loads of learned lumber" were never used, they would still have served the useful purpose of disciplining the mind by cultivating habits of hard mental effort.

If the unity of the educational process had been kept in mind then, great Sunday-school teachers would never have assisted in the organization of the Christian

Endeavor and Leagues and Unions to cultivate the "expressional side" of life while the Sunday school was to cram the mind with biblical information.

In other words, these great leaders were handicapped by the defective psychology and unsatisfactory prevailing educational theories of their day. Given the passion and ability of those leaders between 1870 and 1890, plus the educational science and skill of the year 1920, and the writer believes that an adequate system of church schools for religious instruction might have been achieved in the earlier period. But it was not.

UNREST AND EXPERIMENTATION

The years between 1890 and 1910 were not years of great advance in the evolution of teacher training except in so far as eras of unrest and experimentation may be thus classified. The period of achievement of higher standards must follow the less thrilling but none the less important era of uncertainty, discontent, and experimentation.

Textbooks of 1890-1910.—Between the years just indicated a type of textbook came into existence which was destined to become a "storm center." These books were brief manuals dealing with the Bible, the pupil, the teacher, and the school in as condensed a form as possible. The four authors whose books were most used were Hurlbut, Oliver, Hamill, and Moninger. In some churches teacher training took the form of a "mass movement," whole congregations enrolling for study. Undoubtedly, much good was accomplished where a well-equipped teacher used these works as they were intended to be used, merely as outlines to be supplemented by research and lecturing. But in the main they were not adequate even as guides to the teachers of classes.

In fact, it is difficult to detect in what respect they made much of an advance over the manuals of 1875-1890, prepared by Vincent, Boynton, and others. In both groups of textbooks the aim was to present the information in convenient form so that it might be memorized. The later books perfected the mnemonic devices. They were a complete success as aids to memory. They represented biblical data graphically by diagrams of the fingers of a hand or the spokes of a wheel. They eliminated unnecessary words, so that examination questions calling for a characterization of periods in biblical history could be answered by one word for a period.

Undoubtedly such simplification of material into outline form has merit if the outlines are accompanied by sufficient illustrative materials to enable the students to understand how to use the information. But such was not the case with these books. We find repeated in teacher-training textbooks the mistake previously discovered in the use of the catechism and Uniform Lesson helps. Originally catechisms were but suggestive guides for a teacher; later they became the total curriculum material, and the teacher drilled the student in their memorization. Originally the questions in the lesson helps on the Uniform Lessons were guides for teachers who supplemented the lesson material by outside reading. Later they became the sole support of the teacher, who too frequently degenerated into a drill master.

Dr. Vincent himself originally, as we have noted, did not prepare textbooks but outlines for the normal college, requiring the student to hear lectures based upon the outlines. This seems to have been the general plan from 1867 to 1875. Then textbooks were prepared which elaborated the outlines a very little with no thought that they should contain all the curriculum material of the course. Later textbooks were prepared which simplified the outlines and put them into convenient form for memorizing. Certainly, these textbooks were not intended to constitute all of the curriculum material required for a diploma, but in actual practice they became such far too generally. The examinations were based upon the textbook, and the student memorized the outlines. It was relatively easy for such a student to pass a creditable examination, but he was not prepared to teach because of such memorization.

First standard and advanced standard courses.— The growing feeling against the brief outline studies which we have just described led to the designation of a First Standard and an Advanced Standard Course in 1910. The First Standard was defined to cover approximately what was being offered by the manuals. The Standard called for fifty lessons divided as follows: Bible, twenty; Pupil, seven; Teacher, seven; School, seven; and nine lessons related to any of the above. The course could be finished in one year, but most classes required more than one. A great effort was made to create and popularize a new course of one hundred lessons known as the Advanced Standard Course divided as follows: Bible, forty; Pupil, ten; Teacher, ten; School, ten; Church, ten; Missions, ten; and ten more related to any of the above required subjects. This course was being promoted vigorously by some agencies when the demand for a reappraisal came in 1914, but it never made very serious inroads into the popularity of the manuals which became popularly known as "First Standard" manuals.

Need for revision.—The International Uniform Lessons, 1873, were launched on a floodtide of teacher-training enthusiasm. Undoubtedly, this condition went far toward guaranteeing the success of the new venture. The International Graded Lessons, however, in 1910, had no strong teacher-training current to carry them along. The leading promoters of these lessons and a few like them were well trained and studying faithfully. They had also succeeded in arousing the church and in convincing the people that the curriculum of forty years before was not producing the desired results. This propaganda had spread faster than the leaders anticipated. In fact, the demand for a completely graded course of lessons came before they were ready for it. They had not outlined the lessons and they had not trained the teachers before the clamor for graded lessons became general. In view of this fact the success of the new International Graded Lessons was remarkable. Nevertheless, nothing could be more evident than the need of trained teachers when the Sunday schools were asking for lesson materials based upon the newer psychology and the newer educational theory.

Training courses for primary teachers.—However, it must not be concluded from this general statement that no efforts were being made to train leaders. The organization of the School of Primary Methods at Asbury Park, New Jersey, 1894, and the brilliant record of continuous service rendered by this school, later known as the New Jersey Summer School of Methods, indicates that the primary workers especially were attempting to develop an adequate training program.

The following, which is reproduced from *Quarterly Bulletin of the Primary Department of the International Sunday-School Convention*, January, 1900, page 3ff., will show how one department of the great Sunday-school organization was moving forward in the program of training its teachers:

TEACHER-TRAINING MOVEMENT

REPORT OF CENTRAL COMMITTEE ON TRAINING COURSE FOR PRIMARY TEACHERS

The Need Met.—At the International Convention held last April at Atlanta, Georgia, it was proposed to gratify the long-felt need of the primary teachers for a special course of study to help them in their particular work. It was felt that this would create a definite standard among primary teachers and be a means of educating them for better service. The proposal met with the heartiest approval, and the working out of the plan was committed to the Central Committee of the International Primary Department. This Central Committee met in New York City, November 25, 1899, and outlined the plan which is designated as "Course No. 1."

The Course.—It was the desire of the Committee to present an entirely new course—one which should have been written or compiled with the needs of the primary teacher in view at the time of writing. This was obviously out of the question, in view of the fact that the demand must be met for a course of study at once. Could the Committee have secured the writing or compilation of suitable matter, it would have still further delayed the work, as they would have been unwilling to have commended it for use until tried. However, it is our hope to have such a course in the future. Therefore, the Committee turned their attention to the books already available, and made selections under five heads, as indicated in the outline. In outlining the course they kept in mind the average teacher, the necessity for a simple outline, and the cost of the books.

Training Course for Primary Teachers. Course No. 1

OUTLINE

I. *Bible Study.*—The lessons on the Bible as contained in any one of the following Normal Manuals, viz.:
Hurlbut's, pages 1-69.

149

Legion of Honor, First and Second Series
Pease's, First and Second Year.
Semelroth's.
Worden's.
Dunning's.

Twenty questions will be asked on this Bible study. Ten questions will be general, and ten will be special questions prepared from the Manual chosen by the student. Holders of State Normal certificates or diplomas will be excused from these twenty questions.

II. *Child Study.*—(1) "The Sunday School Teachers' Normal Course," First Year, by George W. Pease. Study pages 121–142.

(2) Read "A Study of Child Nature," by Elizabeth Harrison.

Ten questions will be asked based upon this study.

III. *Laws of Teaching.*—(1) "Normal Courses," First Year, by George W. Pease. Study pages 142–145.

(2) "The Point of Contact in Teaching," by Paterson Du Bois.

Read the whole book.

(3) "Teaching and Teachers," by H. C. Trumbull, D.D.

Read part 1, chapters 1, 2, 3,—pages 1–102.

Eight questions will be asked based upon this study.

IV. *Methods of Teaching.*—(1) "Normal Course," First Year, by George W. Pease. Study Chapters 7, 8, and 9—pages 146–157.

(2) "Teaching and Teachers," by H. C. Trumbull, D.D.

Study Chapter 4, part 1, pages 103–240.

Seven questions will be asked based upon this study.

V. *Methods of Work.*—"Practical Primary Plans," by Israel P. Black.

(1) Study Chapters 1, 14, 17—Class Organization, Grading and Assistants.

(2) Study Chapter 2—Accommodations.

(3) Study Chapters 5, 6—The Class Program.

(4) Study Chapters 15, 20—Home Co-operation.

Five questions will be asked based upon the study of these chapters.

Examination and Diploma.—Fifty questions will comprise the whole examination. When applying for examination papers the student must indicate which special book in the Bible study section was used, that the correct set of questions may be sent. All who pass successfully the examination of Course No. 1, will receive a diploma; this will entitle the holder to study for the seals for advanced courses.

Books Needed for the Training Course

Any of the Normal Outlines, mentioned in Bible Study Section. Average price about........... $0.25

"A Study of Child Nature," Elizabeth Harrison... 1.00

"Sunday School Teacher's Normal Course," First Year, by George W. Pease.................... .25

"The Point of Contact in Teaching," Paterson Du Bois...................................... .40

"Teaching and Teachers," H. C. Trumbull, D.D... 1.00

"Practical Primary Plans," Israel P. Black........ 1.00

This course was promoted zealously by primary workers for several years, but the leaders of the movement themselves will be among the first to admit that the interest in teacher training at this time was in no way commensurate with the need.

Appraisal of standards in 1914.—It is a great organization which can reform itself from within. The International Sunday-School Association and its auxiliaries had been the most vigorous promoters of the older types of First Standard Course. Thousands had enrolled and actually completed these courses under their leadership within recent years. But at the International Sunday-School Convention held in Chicago, 1914, the chairman of their Committee on Education, Professor Walter S. Athearn, discharged all his batteries against the type of course which the Association was promoting so vigorously.

He analyzed the textbooks in minute detail, pointing out how one book discussed the subject of "apperception" in thirteen lines, "memory" in three lines, "imagination" in sixteen, the will in four and a half, while another gave "imagination" nine lines, "memory" twelve lines, and "attention" eighteen. In this latter book "the principles of grading were given in their entirety in eight lines."[15] No answer to Dr. Athearn's indictment was possible except to say, "Yes, they are unsatisfactory according to modern educational standards, but they are the best we can get the people to use, and they are better than nothing." The reply to that was in substance: "We deceive ourselves. We think that we are training teachers by this process when in reality we are simply doing a work which must be done over again if the church ever gets down to the business of doing real school work."

Revision of standards.—In 1915 the Sunday-School Council undertook the revision of teacher-training standards. By agreement it had been understood that the question of standards for use in the local church and the promotion of teacher training in the local church belonged to the denominations, and that the International Sunday-School Association, while assisting the denominations in the promotion of teacher training, would devote the greater part of its attention to the promo-

---

[15] *Religious Education*, December, 1914, p. 545. Published by The Religious Education Association, Chicago

tion of the community aspects of religious education, especially community training schools. The denominations through their representatives in the Council never quite conceded to the International the right to create standards for the community training schools. They never questioned the desirability of having the International and auxiliary associations promote community training schools, but they did question the right to create standards, since these schools were really training teachers and officers for work in a local church. However, in actual practice the Council never quite made clear its policy with reference to community training schools, while the International set high standards in 1914 and maintained them in such schools as sought the right to use an International certificate or diploma.

But in the matter of teacher-training standards for work under the auspices of individual churches the Council proceeded to thoroughly revise the standards. In the first place, it abolished the standards set up for the First Standard and the Advanced Standard Courses, stating that after a given date[16] there should be "only one Standard Course of not less than one hundred and twenty units." A unit was defined as "a recitation period of not less than forty-five minutes based upon a lesson assignment by an approved author, the lesson assignment to require a minimum of one hour for lesson preparation."

New standards.—The new course required not less than one hundred and twenty lessons and the allotment of lessons was as follows:

---

[16] Determined by the denominations individually; several set January 1, 1917. as the date.

Year I	Year II	Year III
The Pupil, 10 units.	Teaching Values of Old Testament, 10 units.	Specialization in the Methods of a particular department, 40 units.
The Teacher, 10 units.	Training of the Devotional Life, 10 units.	
Teaching Values of the Life of Christ, 10 units.	Teaching Values of New Testament, 10 units.	
Organization and Administration of the Sunday School, 10 units.	The Program of the Christian religion, 10 units.	

It will be noted that the new Standard Course was considerably longer than the Advanced Standard Course and very much longer than the First Standard. However, this longer course was made more usable by being divided into short sections. Textbooks were prepared especially for each section. These textbooks tried to cover only a small portion of the entire field, but to do so with enough elaboration to guide the student in a use of the principles set forth. Bible-content material was practically eliminated from the course as outlined on the assumption that this was being adequately presented in the graded lessons, but a study of curriculum values in the Bible was given especial consideration, as the following subjects will show: "Teaching Values in the Life of Christ"—Year I; "Teaching Values in the Old Testament," "Teaching Values in the New Testament," Year II.

The purpose of the creators of these standards was to present material that is common for the training of all Sunday-school workers in the first two years with specialization in the methods of a particular department, including observation and practice, in the third year. Several syndicate groups were formed for the preparation of textbooks to meet the Standards of the first two years, but the leading denominational agencies formed one syndicate for the publication of the "specialization" books of the third year.

Denominational Courses.—The Council determined standards but did not outline courses. However, the Teacher Training Committee of the Council did unofficially offer some outlines to publishers. It was understood that the various denominations could prepare their own outlines and publish their own textbooks as long as the main features of the standard were met. The Methodist Episcopal Church and the Methodist Episcopal Church, South, cooperated with the other denominations in the preparation of standards, and even of outlines, but in the preparation of textbooks these two, in cooperation, published an independent series. In this series they have attempted to build upon the curriculum of the International Graded Lessons, Berean Series, up to and including the twelfth grade (17th year). Following this year the courses were planned so as to prepare the students for definite skill in the performance of their Christian tasks. The first year of this course offers *Life in the Making*, 24 units; *Learning and Teaching*, 24 units. The second year contains four short courses: *The Training of the Devotional Life*, 12 units; *The Organization and Administration of the Sunday School*, 12 units; *The Program of the Christian Religion*, 12 units; and *A Methodist Church and Its Work*, 12 units. In the third, or specialization, year the syndicate courses will be used.

MEANS FOR TEACHER TRAINING

The prevailing means for the training of teachers of religion are:

1. Training classes in the local church.

2. Community training schools.
3. Training by correspondence.
4. Training institutes.
5. Summer training schools.
6. Training in higher institutions of learning.

The denominational agencies have given special attention to 1, 3, 4, 5, 6. The International Association and its auxiliaries have devoted the greater part of their attention to 2, 4, and 5, although such State associations as that of Pennsylvania have been active in the promotion of "1." Out of 130,000 students enrolled for training in the Methodist Episcopal Church since the organization of its Teacher Training Department in 1909, at least two thirds of these have been in classes conducted by the local church. Other denominations would report a similar percentage. In fact, a program of training in the local church is favored by all of the agencies for the promotion of religious education.

The community training school movement has not yet reached the stage of development that the training class system in the local church has reached. Community projects are harder to get under way and to keep going than projects which enlist a more homogeneous constituency. Nevertheless, it seems to be clear that there is great need for a nation-wide chain of community training schools to supplement the efforts of the individual churches, and especially to train a constituency of parents and workers who will support the community week-day schools of religion. And, fortunately, there are enough community training schools which have done successful work for several years to warrant our considering the plan an assured success instead of an experiment. *The City Institute for Re-*

ligious Teachers, Athearn, is one of the few books on the subject, but excellent pamphlets have been published about "The Malden Plan," "The Evanston School," and others. Saint Louis, Cleveland, New York, and other cities have conducted these schools successfully for several years.[17]

Training by correspondence.—Correspondence courses for the training of religious workers have not yet been developed as generally as one might expect, considering the popularity of the method as promoted by such agencies as the International Correspondence School, the Moody Bible Institute, and State normal and agricultural schools. The Board of Sunday Schools of the Methodist Episcopal Church launched such an enterprise in 1909, and published the textbooks of the Worker and Work Series especially prepared for these courses. Six thousand students have enrolled for these courses since 1909, and the results in the lives of the students have more than justified the enterprise. To-day courses are offered by this agency not only for teachers and superintendents in every department of the Sunday school from Cradle Roll to Adult, but also for general superintendents and for supervisors of teaching, of missions, of worship and evangelism, of recreation, of records, and of finance. There is a future of large usefulness in this field for any agency which has the funds sufficient to advertise widely and to employ the required number of able instructors. But the Methodists have never had large funds to invest in this field. The Moody Bible Institute offers correspondence courses for Sunday-school teachers, but does

---

[17] Educational Bulletin numbers 6, 7, 8, 1918, issued by International Sunday-School Association, present the subject of standards and materials for these schools. Bulletins published by Boston University and Northwestern University deal with "The Malden Plan" and "The Evanston School."

very little in the field of Sunday school methods, specializing particularly on Bible study.

Training Institutes.—These institutes vary in length all the way from one afternoon to a period lasting three or six weeks. Both the denominational and the International Association agencies use the institute plan. On the whole, within the last ten years even the one and two-day institutes have been very helpful in giving to workers the general principles underlying modern work in religious education together with practical hints for the applications of these principles. The one-week "Standard Training Schools" as developed by the Methodist Episcopal Church, South, have given training of a very high order. But the longer Summer Schools of Religious Education, usually held for about ten days, as developed by all the agencies indicated above, have been the most successful training projects yet undertaken in this field. The faculties of these summer schools are made up of professors and executives of international reputation in this field. The student is limited to a certain number of courses and is required to do written work or pass an examination before receiving credit toward the certificate awarded.

New Jersey summer school.—One of the pioneers that blazed the way for the summer schools was the New Jersey Summer School, founded in 1895 by E. Morris Fergusson, then the State secretary for New Jersey and to-day State secretary for Massachusetts. He founded it for the express purpose of bringing together the workers who desired better lesson materials and better methods. If one will compare the personnel of the Graded Lessons Conference and the writers of the courses of the International Graded Lessons with the names of those most zealous in promoting the school at

Asbury Park in the years 1906–1914, he will see how closely associated these groups were and how much one contributed to the other. Among the names common to both groups are: Mrs. J. Woodbridge Barnes, Frances Danielson, Marion Thomas, Josephine L. Baldwin, Milton S. Littlefield, E. Morris Fergusson, Sidney A. Weston, Ralph E. Diffendorfer, and Arlo Ayres Brown. Many a summer school owes its birth to the success of the New Jersey Summer School.

Training in higher institutions.—Since a later chapter will deal specifically with the training of teachers in higher institutions of learning, we will defer consideration of the subject at this time.

Achievement in promoting teacher training.—All agencies promoting Sunday-school work make some attempt to stimulate teacher training. And yet the fact remains that no local church, however creditable its record, has yet given enough attention to training to insure competent leadership for its present and future needs. And no general agency, for the promotion of religious education has ever invested either time or money enough in this movement to expect success. Nevertheless, some agencies have worked faithfully along this line and with encouraging results.

The Pennsylvania State Sunday-School Association reports through the Rev. Charles A. Oliver that since he became superintendent of the teacher-training work of the Association in February, 1901, the Association has enrolled 163,348 students and has awarded 53,716 diplomas. He adds the following comment: "All the enrolled students except perhaps four or five hundred have taken a first standard course. With a few exceptions those taking advanced work took the preliminary work of the first standard course and followed that with advanced work. They were not enrolled again. In 1921 we enrolled 8,020 new students. All but a very few registering with us are taking a first standard course, and a good percentage go on to more thorough work for seals."

The Southern Baptist Convention through its Sunday-School Board has also made a remarkable record. This agency does not keep a record of students enrolled but of awards which are given on the "incomplete diploma plan." The following is taken from its report for the year 1921:

INCREASE BY YEARS

	Diplomas	Red Seals	Blue Seals	Post Graduates	Gold Seals
Before 1914.......	22,601	2,512	1,298	...	...
1914.............	4,559	1,088	625	40	0
1915.............	4,565	1,077	474	210	75
1916.............	5,694	1,144	493	146	77
1917.............	6,426	1,341	676	195	95
1918.............	5,770	1,320	548	189	120
1919.............	6,440	1,455	617	154	91
1920.............	9,938	2,259	930	330	207
1921.............	17,011	3,288	1,434	517	269
Total.........	83,004	15,484	7,095	1,781	934

TEACHER TRAINING BOOKS COMPLETED DURING 1921

In institutes and training schools......................	7,511
In schools and colleges...............................	11,745
In local classes.....................................	22,366
By individual examinations............................	5,962
In postgraduate study................................	2,167
Total Book Awards, 1921...........................	49,751

The Board of Sunday Schools of the Methodist Episcopal Church organized its Department of Teacher Training under the leadership of Wade Crawford Barclay in 1909. The writer succeeded Dr. Barclay in 1914 and remained through the greater part of the year 1921.

Since 1909 this agency has enrolled in classes 132,863 students of whom 19,699 were enrolled in 1921. Other agencies are also meeting with great success. The year 1921 seems to have closed with more people studying to prepare themselves for leadership in religious education than ever before. It will be understood that while teacher training is the main emphasis in the movement which we have described in this chapter, the training of administrative officers is also included under the general title.

SUMMARY

We have noted the haphazard efforts to train teachers of religion prior to 1860, and then the very definite effort to keep pace with the movement for the training of public-school teachers. We have seen how a new era of religious training seemed to dawn between 1865 and 1890. The enthusiasm for Bible study and the earnest efforts of the International Sunday-School Association workers seemed certain to revolutionize the churches. But we were compelled to note that this era of enthusiasm and great beginnings failed to measure up to expectations. Then we noted an era of unrest and experimentation followed by the introduction of International Graded Lessons and a new movement for the training of teachers.

The limitations of the present plans and materials for the training of officers and teachers we recognize. Nevertheless, it is gratifying to note that more people are studying to prepare themselves for teaching religion than ever before and that the materials used are more scientifically organized and better adapted to this purpose than ever before. It would seem as if this era of training were just at the dawn instead of having passed the midday of achievement. There is every reason for expecting in the near future that the leading Christian educators of many communities will unite their forces in community training programs, while the individual churches will continue to arouse and to train their constituencies for better service. Also there is every reason to expect that the colleges and universities at last will accept as one of their tasks the preparation of students for this much-needed form of social service. If these movements continue to make headway the dreams of Vincent, Eggleston, Trumbull, and others may become a reality in the first half of the twentieth century.

Topics for discussion:

1. How do you account for the rise of normal schools for the training of public-school teachers about the middle of the nineteenth century? Analyze and evaluate the factors which contributed to this rise.
2. How much progress had been made in teacher training for public-school service prior to the Civil War? To what extent had this influenced Sunday-school teaching?
3. Compare such teacher-training books as, *The Teacher Taught*, *The Sunday-School Teacher's Guide*, and *The Sabbath School Index* with textbooks accredited in the present "Standard Course."
4. Compare the textbooks prepared by Vincent, Boynton, and others of the period 1870–1890 with those prepared by Hurlbut, Oliver, Moninger, and Hamill, 1890–1910, and then with those of the present "Standard Course."

5. What was the permanent value of the great "teachers' meetings" of twenty to thirty years ago?

6. Would the cause of religious education have been advanced if the Chautauqua Movement had confined its attention to the training of teachers for religious education?

7. Why did the impetus for teacher training that was so marked from 1870 to 1890 not continue to gather momentum until the close of the period? What were the permanent contributions to the materials and technique of teacher training made in this period?

8. What are the merits and defects of the present teacher-training textbooks which are most commonly used?

Brief bibliography for special references:

Cubberley—*Public Education in the United States.* Houghton Mifflin Company, Boston, 1919.

(No author named) *The Teacher Taught.* American Sunday-School Union, 1839.

Kidder—*The Sunday School Teachers' Guide.* Lane & Tippett, New York, 1848.

Pardee—*The Sabbath-School Index.* J. C. Garrigues & Co., Philadelphia, 1869.

Inglis—*The Sabbath School and Bible Teaching.* Lane & Scott, New York, 1850.

Vincent—*The Sunday-School Teachers' Institution.* Adams, Blackmer, and Lyon, Chicago, 1866.

Vincent—*The Church School and Normal Guide.* Hunt & Eaton, New York, 1889.

Normal Class Manual, published by The Bible and Education Society, Philadelphia, 1873.

Hurlbut—*The Story of Chautauqua*. G. P. Putnam's Sons, New York, 1921.

Hurlbut—*Revised Normal Lessons*. Revision of *Outline Normal Lessons*, 1885. Eaton & Mains, New York, 1907.

Hurlbut—*Teacher Training Lessons for the Sunday School*. Eaton & Mains, New York, 1908.

Oliver—*Preparation for Teaching*. The Westminster Press, Philadelphia, 1908.

McElfresh—*The Training of Sunday-School Teachers and Officers*. Eaton & Mains, New York, 1914.

Weigle—*The Pupil and the Teacher*. Copyright by The Lutheran Publication Society. George H. Doran Company, New York, 1911.

Athearn—*The Church School*. The Pilgrim Press, Boston, 1911.

Barclay-Brown et al.—*Life in the Making*. The Methodist Book Concern, New York, 1917.

New Standard Teacher-Training Textbooks as used by any denomination.

CHAPTER VII

BRIEF ACCOUNT OF PROMOTIONAL AGENCIES OF RELIGIOUS EDUCATION

IT is not enough to invent or create an instrument for the benefit of the race; some one must promote the use of the instrument, if it is ever to be effective.

EARLIEST PROMOTERS OF THE MODERN SUNDAY SCHOOL

Robert Raikes, as we have noted, was not the first even in his own day to use a Sunday school to aid the young in religion and morals. But he was the first in his day to give publicity to the plan and to seek to promote it. He first gave publicity to his schools in 1783, and as early as 1785 the Sunday-School Society was formed for the promotion of Sunday schools. This society carried on successful work promoting Sunday schools for several years and was succeeded by The Sunday-School Union, formed in London, 1803. This Union has had a long career of successful Sunday-school promotion, including in its work improvements in lesson materials and methods, aggressive missionary work, and the publishing of literature.[1]

In America the earliest religious schools were the community day schools, in which, as we have noted, the religious materials constituted so large a part of the curriculum. An occasional use of Sunday sessions for teaching religion to the young has also been noted, but there was no marked movement toward the development of Sunday schools until after the War for American

[1] See article on Sunday Schools in England, from Robert Raikes' Onward, *The Encyclopedia of Sunday Schools of Religious Education*, Volume III. Published by Thomas Nelson & Sons, New York, 1915.

Independence and after the Raikes plan had been made known.

Wesley in England was an immediate supporter of Sunday schools as soon as Robert Raikes gave publicity to his plan. He saw the possibility of making these schools "nurseries of the faith," and, with his genius for organization, he promoted them along with his "societies." In 1790 the Minutes of the Methodist Conference report what is probably the first official recognition of Sunday schools by an American general church organization.[2]

We have already noted the organization in December, 1790, of the first society in America for the promotion of Sunday schools, the slow development prior to the War of 1812, and the great revival of interest in religion and education which followed the termination of this war. We discussed also the rise of city unions such as those in New York, Boston, and Philadelphia.[3]

American Sunday-School Union.—In 1824 these city unions were merged into one organization, the American Sunday-School Union, the most influential Sunday-school organization on the continent for approximately the next fifty years. Or perhaps it would be more exact to say that the Sunday-and-Adult School Union of Philadelphia developed into this larger organization with the other city unions cooperating. America can never repay the debt which it owes to the American Sunday-School Union. Founded by laymen, with its governing board[4] excluding any but laymen, it nevertheless had the hearty cooperation of the ministers who were most vitally interested in Sunday-

---

[2] See Chapter III, p. 49.

[3] See Chapter III, p. 50.

[4] Rice—*The Sunday-School Movement and the American Sunday-School Union, 1817–1917*, p. 82. The American Sunday-School Union. Used by permission.

school progress.[5] And it pioneered in this field when most of the denominations were hesitating over whether to promote the use of Sunday for religious instruction or to oppose such as Sabbath desecration.

The Union prepared lesson books, reading libraries, and other Sunday-school literature as required. It financed and supervised the planting of new schools in the West and wherever there was the greatest need. In many places where the Sunday-school missionary founded schools and aided them there were neither churches nor day schools. Such missionaries as Stephen A. Paxson, and others, left behind them a record of which any society might well be proud. How much the new Middle-Western States owed to these brave Sunday-school missionaries and the early frontier preachers can never be estimated.

The Union has in recent years confined its attention largely to the establishment of mission schools, and to the publication of literature for small schools. While it has not influenced the educational policies of the Sunday-school world as largely since 1874 as it did in the first fifty years of its existence, it is to-day a strong, useful agency for the dissemination of Sunday-school literature and the establishment of new Sunday schools in rural and especially in neglected sections of the country. Its annual report for the year ended February 28, 1922, shows an income of $545,116.64, and a total expenditure of $576,813.90, divided as follows: Publication Department, $161,312.29; Missionary Department, $361,365.21; General, $54,136.40.   Excess of expenses, etc., over income, $31,697.26.[6]

---

[5] The executive officials have been clergymen.

[6] The One Hundred and Fifth Annual Report of the American Sunday-School Union (the ninety-eighth under its present name), 1922, p. 22.

National Sunday-school conventions.—The first "National Sunday-school convention,"[7] so called, was held in 1832, and grew out of a conference held in Philadelphia during the anniversary meeting of the American Sunday-School Union, and the session of the General Assembly of the Presbyterian Church, May 23, 1832. Here the members of the conference caught a vision of the possibilities of a convention which should assemble delegates from all parts of America for the discussion of Sunday-school problems. They issued a call for such a convention and appointed a committee which prepared a questionnaire to be sent to Sunday-school workers all over the land and to form the basis for the discussions of the conventions. Three hundred answers to this questionnaire were received and the First National Convention which was held in New York city in the Chatham Street Chapel, October 3, 4, 5, 1832, was a very successful one. Two hundred twenty delegates were present, representing fourteen of the twenty-four States and four Territories of the Union. So enthusiastic were the delegates over the success of this meeting that they voted to call another in the following year. But it came too soon and did not attract such wide attention. The Third National Convention was not held until February 22–24, 1859.

The war interrupted the rising tide of Sunday-school interest and the next national convention was not held until April 28, 1869, in Newark, New Jersey. Of this meeting the editor of *The Sunday-School Times* said: "Never before had so many Sunday-school leaders of the land been brought face to face. Taken as a whole,

---

[7] *Organized Sunday-School Work in America, 1908–1911.* Official Report of the Thirteenth International Sunday-School Convention, San Francisco, California, 1911, pp. 11ff.

it was the most memorable Sunday-school gathering ever assembled in the United States, if not in the world. Tongues of fire seemed to be given to the speakers. The spirit of brotherly love and union prevailed. It was estimated that there were over twenty-five hundred visitors, in addition to the five hundred twenty-six delegates, in attendance."[8]

The Fifth National Convention, held at Indianapolis, 1872, is memorable in that it declared in favor of a system of Uniform Bible Lessons for all ages in the Sunday school, and created a lesson committee that was international because it included two members from Canada.

International Sunday-School Conventions.—The Sixth National was also the First International Sunday-School Convention held in Baltimore, May 11–13, 1875. Twenty Canadian representatives participated in its proceedings. From that time on International Sunday-School Conventions were held every three years up to and including the Fourteenth International Convention in Chicago in 1914, when the period of convention intervals was changed to four years.

Organization of the International Sunday-School Association.—For many years the international Sunday-school movement had no incorporated organization. It was guided through conventions, and the development of a permanent organization was slow. The first salaried officer was a statistical secretary, E. Payson Porter, elected by the Convention in 1872. His salary was paid for a time by the Illinois Sunday-School Association, later the *Sunday-School Times* assisting. The Executive Committee of the Convention which in 1907 became the incorporated International Sunday-School Association was organized by the Convention of 1881. B. F. Jacobs, to whom the Sunday-school world owes so much, was the first chairman and continued in this capacity until his death in 1902. The first official organizer for the international field was William Reynolds, of Illinois, elected as "Field Superintendent" by the Convention of 1887. He was assisted from time to time by such men as Professor H. M. Hamill and others who were loaned by State Associations. In the Convention of 1899 at Atlanta, Marion Lawrance, of Ohio, was elected as general secretary and the association began to build up a staff of full-time paid workers. The incorporation came in 1907 through a charter granted by the Congress of the United States.[9]

The limitations of this book do not permit a detailed study of the activities of the International Sunday-School Association and of the tremendous influence of its leaders who have so successfully guided this organized interdenominational Sunday-school movement. The narrative of this influence is interwoven with that of all the Sunday-school activities since 1872.

Organized State Sunday-School Associations.— Very great influence has been wielded by the State Sunday-school Associations which have been auxiliary to the International Sunday-School Association but independent of it in management. In fact, the international movement is clearly the outgrowth of the successful State developments. The first wholly self-managed, self-perpetuating, County Sunday-school Convention was that organized in Scott County, Illinois, April 20, 1846, by Stephen Paxson. H. Clay Trumbull, another pioneer in organization, became county secretary of Hartford County, Connecticut Convention,

---

[9] *Encyclopedia of Sunday Schools and Religious Education.*

about 1856, while in 1858 New Jersey held its first State Convention. But the most significant record for organizing a State is that held by B. F. Jacobs, William Reynolds, Dwight L. Moody, assisted by other brilliant leaders, who set out to organize every county in the State of Illinois so that it would have a county secretary and an annual county convention. In 1865 they had one hundred and two counties in line.

The State Associations have developed until, including their county and township organizations, they have to-day approximately two hundred seventy-five paid full-time workers in the United States and Canada. Some conception of the strength of this work may be formed by considering the following facts: In 1921 the New York State Sunday-School Association alone employed five full-time staff workers with six stenographers at the central office and twenty full-time division workers under the able leadership of Joseph Clark, general superintendent. In Pennsylvania eight State workers were employed on a budget of $60,570; in addition to four employed by the Philadelphia Sunday-School Association with its annual budget of $20,000.

These auxiliary associations pay a small percentage of their income annually to the International Sunday-School Association, looking to the latter for guidance in the formulation of standards and programs, but otherwise each is independent of the authority of the other except for considerable interlocking in the executive committees of the International and of the State organizations. Until 1920 these associations, International and State, maintained their work independent of any official approval by any of the large denominations and without any official representation of the denominations upon their executive committees. The idea of the Sunday school as a layman's movement independent of any denominational authority was held through all these years by the majority of leaders within the conventions and the executive committees. Of the administrative staff of the International, numbering twelve in 1921, all were laymen with but one exception, and this has been the rule throughout its history. On the other hand, while the State associations have been controlled by laymen, many State general secretaries have been clergymen.

THE WORLD'S SUNDAY-SCHOOL ASSOCIATION

The World's Sunday-School Association began as a World's Sunday-School Convention, which was held in London in 1889. The convention was the result of conferences and a desire for cooperation between a group of American Sunday-school leaders active in the International Sunday-School Association and such British Sunday-school men as Sir Francis Flint Belsey, the Rev. Carey Bonner, the Rt. Hon. Lord Kinnaird, and Sir John Kirk. Prominent in the American group were: B. F. Jacobs, William Reynolds, Dr. Duncan, E. K. Warren, J. H. Vincent, Marion Lawrance, E. Morris Fergusson, and Joseph Clark.

That convention was made up chiefly of delegates from Great Britain and America. The American delegates chartered a ship, the Bothnia, for the overseas journey. The decision to extend the organized Sunday-school work to India was the chief result of the convention.

The second convention was held in Saint Louis in 1893, as a part of the International Sunday-School Convention. Dr. Phillips, secretary for India, was moved there to make a plea for the Sunday-school work in Japan. Several hundred dollars were pledged for this, and a Japanese worker, a Mr. Ikehara, was later engaged for service in the Empire.

The third convention was also held in London in 1898, the extension of the Sunday-school organization to the continent of Europe being the chief result of this convention. In 1904 the Fourth World's Convention was held in Jerusalem, and developed a great passion for the extension of Sunday-school work in mission fields. In 1907 the Fifth World's Convention assembled in Rome. En route to Rome many of the delegates visited cities in North Africa and became so enthusiastic over the missionary possibilities in that part of the world that they pledged generous support to Bishop Joseph C. Hartzell if the Methodist Episcopal Church would undertake work in that field. The result of the Convention was that the missionary vision of the leaders was still further broadened and a great impetus given to a world-wide Sunday-school program. It was at Rome that the convention became organized as a World's Sunday-School Association.

At the Sixth World's Convention, in Washington, 1910, the Association definitely undertook a program of larger executive responsibility by electing Mr. Marion Lawrance as general secretary to give part time to the World's Association as well as to the International Association. The Seventh Convention, held in Zurich, 1913, was attended by 2,609 delegates including 221 missionaries, and representing 51 countries and 75 denominations. It was at this convention that six great commissions reported as to the Sunday-school conditions and needs of the world.

The last convention, held in Tokyo, 1920, was

especially significant for two reasons: first, it gave to the churches of Protestantism in Great Britain, Canada, the United States, and other nations a unique opportunity to express unitedly their ideal of a Christian world brotherhood when such a statement was greatly needed. Second, it brought inspiration and information on Sunday-school work to the Far East in a powerful way. Convention delegates spoke not only in Japan, China, Korea, and the Philippines, but some of them returned home by way of Malaysia, India, and Egypt in order to make whatever contribution they could to Sunday-school work in those countries.

Program and influence of the Association.—As we should expect in organizations deriving their authority from a popular convention meeting once every few years, the Executive Committee becomes practically the working organization. For the first twenty-one years the main business of this Association was the holding of conventions, but in 1910, at the Washington Convention, being impressed with the urgency of the need for Sunday-school work in various parts of the world, the Association undertook the financing of Sunday-school missionaries in distant lands.

Marion Lawrance and Frank L. Brown.—Marion Lawrance was the first general secretary of the World's Sunday-School Association, but in 1910 he asked to have Frank L. Brown associated with him. In 1914 Mr. Lawrance resigned, and Mr. Brown remained as general secretary. In 1921 Mr. W. C. Pearce, long a conspicuous leader in the International Association work, became an associate general secretary. Mr. Brown was a layman who for thirty-six years had been the superintendent of the Sunday school of Bushwick Avenue Central Methodist Episcopal Church, of

Brooklyn, New York. He was a chairman of a committee which in 1886 founded the school with only eighty members. It grew to a membership of three thousand five hundred in 1914, and is to-day one of the greatest Sunday schools in America, not only in membership, but also in educational efficiency. His practical Sunday-school experience, together with his executive ability and rare spirit, made him a very successful leader. His distinguished services were terminated by death in 1922.[10] In recording the work of this Association one should not fail to mention such distinguished American laymen as the late E. K. Warren, Dr. George W. Bailey, H. J. Heinz, James W. Kinnear, and the late president, the Hon. John Wanamaker—men who by their breadth of vision and generous financial contributions have done so much for the movement.

Organization.[11]—The work of the Association between conventions is carried on by an Executive Committee of one hundred and twenty members. Sixty of these are located in America, and sixty in various countries. Of the sixty in America twelve are appointed by the Foreign Missions Conference of North America, six by the Sunday-School Council of Evangelical Denominations, and six by the International Sunday-School Association.[12] The balance are additional representative church leaders and laymen. The sixty members in other countries are nominated by the various Unions

---

[10] W. G. Landes, formerly General Secretary of the Pennsylvania State Sunday-School Association, has been elected to succeed the late Mr. Frank L. Brown.

[11] The writer is indebted for information concerning the policies and program of the World's Sunday-School Association to personal letters from the late Mr. Frank L. Brown.

[12] The method of selecting the last twelve will be changed by the merger of the two organizations named into the International Sunday-School Council of Religious Education.

or Associations affiliated with the World's Association. These Unions or Associations in each field are governed by committees representing the mission and church bodies on the field.

Since 1900 Sunday-School Associations, Unions, or committees, in affiliation with the World's Sunday-School Association, have been promoted in thirty-seven countries and the number is constantly increasing. It is the plan of the World's Association to vitally and, when possible, organically relate these affiliated Associations, Unions, or committees to the existing missions and church organizations in each field.

Sunday-school missionaries or specialists supported by the Association are trained and equipped in the homeland and then sent to the field and placed under the direction of the responsible national Sunday-school organization, to produce literature, train leaders, hold institutes, and promote standards.

In some fields competent Sunday-school denominational specialists are loaned to the interdenominational work and the budget is furnished by the World's Association. In every field employed denominational Sunday-school men, native or missionary, work in close relationship to the interdenominational Sunday-school program in order to avoid inefficiency, duplication, and waste.

The quadrennial convention is now incidental to the work of the Association which aims to gird the whole world with a chain of Sunday-school organizations having trained secretaries in each field, in order to promote continental visitations by specialists, to develop in each field Bible lessons and Sunday-school literature indigenous to the field, to train a native Sunday-school leadership and to extend the Sunday school as one of the chief factors in Christian education, church membership, world evangelization, and world brotherhood.

THE RELIGIOUS EDUCATION ASSOCIATION

Before discussing the rise of denominational Sunday-school boards let us consider an organization which has never undertaken large executive responsibilities, but which nevertheless has exerted a great influence upon religious education during the last eighteen years.

In 1903 a meeting was called in Chicago for the purpose of considering the condition of religious education in the United States and the best means of developing this vital movement. It drew to its sessions some of the most forward-looking men and women in the church, especially those who had a burning conviction concerning the importance of arousing the church to a better appreciation of the necessity for religious education.

Since then the Religious Education Association, which was organized at that meeting, or the Council of Religious Education, a part of the Association, has met once a year for the discussion of various problems in this field. While this organization has had no organic relation to any church, its governing board has always contained a majority of clergymen who are conspicuous in their denominations. These men have not feared being known as radical in the field of religious education and have exerted themselves in the task of investigating and making known the experiments in this field and the factors essential to success. The magazine, *Religious Education*, published by the Association, has been a powerful factor in molding public opinion.

The constitution of the Religious Education Association declares its object to be: "To inspire the educational forces of our country with the religious ideal, to inspire the religious forces of our country with the educational ideal, and to keep before the public mind the ideal of religious education, and the sense of its need and value."

The scope of the Association will be noted when we call attention to the fact that at its meeting at Rochester, March, 1921, the convention met in the following sections:

Directors of Religious Education.

Department of Universities and Colleges.

Department of Bible Teachers in Colleges.

Department of Church Schools.

Department of Churches and Pastors.

Department of Public Schools.

Department of Theological Seminaries.

Department of Community Agencies.

Influence of the Religious Education Association. —It is yet too soon to adequately estimate the influence of the Religious Education Association. In the early years of its organization it was perhaps the most potent single factor in crystallizing the sentiment in favor of better methods in religious education. It brought together men and women from many denominations, representing many theories and viewpoints in education, but all agreeing that the church was not taking seriously enough her task of religious training and not utilizing for this training the most approved educational materials and methods.

In addition to the valuable findings of its several commissions, what this Association has prompted others to do will be perhaps its chief glory. However, it has not only started forward movements but has kept in the forefront of the general movement by investigating and publishing the results of its investigations of any enterprise which seemed to be most significant.

Henry F. Cope, general secretary since 1907, has written many stimulating books on various subjects in this field and has been a very helpful factor not only in the success of his organization but in the development of better methods and materials. The topic of its convention in 1922, "Week-Day Religious Instruction in America," shows to what extent it is still a leader. The subject has been before the Association repeatedly since 1915, but at this session it was made the main theme, and the meeting proved to be one of the most helpful in the history of the Association.

RISE OF DENOMINATIONAL INTEREST

The rise of denominational interest in Sunday-school work since 1905 has been the most significant feature in the history of religious education in the last forty years. If the writer were asked to indicate three outstanding events in the Sunday-school history of America, he would name the organization of the American Sunday-School Union, 1824; the organization of the International Lesson Committee, 1872; and the reorganization of the International Sunday-School Association so as to provide for denominational cooperation, 1921. Strangely enough, approximately fifty years intervened between each event, and, as we should expect, each event is but the culmination of several years of experimentation and zealous promotion.

INFLUENCE OF PESTALOZZI, FROEBEL, AND HERBART

The influence of the normal schools in public education was felt by the Sunday-school world as early as 1860, but the public schools of America themselves did not really apply in any large way the principles set forth by Pestalozzi, Froebel, and Herbart until about 1890, although these principles were known to Americans in the first half of the century when they were being worked out by these great educational pioneers.

The writer was fortunate enough to be a student in the practice school at Normal, Illinois, when Charles McMurray and other Herbartionists were practicing their theories. Instead of the older type of "reader" we read real literature, such as *Lays of Ancient Rome*, Macaulay, in the sixth grade, and Shakespearian plays in the seventh and eighth. Appeal was made to the interests of the class in the teaching of reading, grammar, geography, and other subjects. Pupils were advanced as soon as they were competent to do the work in a higher class regardless of the time of year when this discovery was made. Study could be done either at home or in the schoolroom. Some classes recited out of doors occasionally. In every way the student was stimulated to think for himself and to act upon his own initiative.

Schools with such discipline are common to-day, but in the early nineties they were pioneers in America. A society of Herbartionists was formed for the propagation of these educational principles. The liberalizing of the curriculum was a necessary sequence of directing so much attention to the interests of the pupil.

The story of this advance in public school methods belongs in another history, but the parallel advance in religious educational methods must be noted here. The Sunday school did not require as much time to apply the modern theories after they were used in the public school world as the public school took to use them after they were first promoted by Pestalozzi and Froebel. In fact as soon as the newer viewpoint and methods had been accepted in leading public school circles the Sunday-school workers began to take note and to plan accordingly.

Effect of new principles upon the curriculum.— The curriculum is the stronghold of the conservatives. Perhaps the fact that so much of curriculum material has been selected from the experience of the past may be a partial explanation. But, in any event, even after thirty years of emphasis upon preparing the pupil for social efficiency by fitting the curriculum material to his immediate needs and interests, both high schools and colleges not uncommonly require an amount of work in some subjects out of all proportion to the needs of the individual and of the society in which he is to serve.

It is not unfair nor derogatory to their organizations to say that the leaders of the International Sunday-School Association and also of the International Lesson Committee were conservative on curriculum matters between 1890 and 1914. If the denominational Sunday-school agencies had been strong organizations employing large and influential staffs between the years of 1890–1910, they might also have been found on the conservative side. But the denominations were just awaking to the importance of religious education and to its possibilities in the light of recent educational practice. Fortunately, several of the leading editors were demanding a new day. The new educational movements appealed to denominational workers who had no precedents to which they were attached. The awakening interest in better educational methods, the splendid creative work in public school and general education, the influence of pioneers such as William Rainey Harper, George Albert Coe, and others who helped to launch the Religious Education Association, the widespread discontent over inadequate results in Sunday schools—all these, with many other factors, inspired the churches to undertake an aggressive campaign for Sunday-school improvement.

To the credit of the International Sunday-School Association, let it be said that this body kept itself in the advance through the conference called by W. N. Hartshorne in Boston, 1907, and the instruction of the convention to the lesson committee in 1908 to prepare a system of completely graded lessons. But there were radical differences of opinion as to what curriculum material these graded lessons should contain. "The Bible only" had been the prevailing opinion since 1872, but the failure of the International Uniform Lesson System, in recent years at least, to produce a generation which knew how to use the Bible in everyday life made the more radical elements feel that other materials in proper proportions should be introduced. They held the view that, while the Bible is the great source book for religious education, church history, God's work in nature, missionary achievements, and other subjects should be introduced in order to develop men and women who are competent to do their work in society.

Had conditions been reversed, had the denominational societies been the long-established agencies of Sunday-school promotion, they probably would have defended the past while the laymen of some newly formed society would have been the radicals. But the fact is that the laymen, aided by a few influential ministers, were in power, and they determined to hold to the principles which had won victory for them. Therefore the denominations felt that they must organize and promote for themselves if the newer methods were to have a chance in their churches.

RISE OF THE SUNDAY-SCHOOL COUNCIL OF EVANGELICAL DENOMINATIONS

The writer is not criticizing the men and women on either side. He is simply saying that between 1908 and 1914 a "battle royal" was on in the Sunday-school world. The battle was for principles and not for personal advantage. Had men been considering their own comfort and popularity, the outcome would have been different. They felt that they were crusaders battling for the faith, and battling for the rights of childhood. The spirit of the controversy was to a remarkable extent above reproach. Men tried to be fair and conscientious whether winning or losing. The outcome in curriculum matters was the International Graded Lessons, and in organization a new society for the promotion of Sunday-school work known as the Sunday-School Council of Evangelical Denominations, organized in 1910. This new organization was composed of the official representatives of the several denominational agencies for Sunday-school promotion, the editors and publishers being at this time the strongly predominating element.

Reorganization of the International Lesson Committee.—After some unpleasant antagonism between the International Sunday-School Association, allied with its auxiliary State and provincial associations, and the Sunday-School Council of Evangelical Denominations, allied with its denominational constituencies, the two groups began to understand each other better and to move toward a common program. The first step toward this was the reorganization of the International Lesson Committee in 1914 making a lesson committee of three sections—"a" the International section of eight members, formerly the entire committee, "b" the Sunday-School Council section of eight members, "c" one representative for each denomination having a general Sunday-school curriculum committee. At the session of the committee, December 29, 1920, this third section was composed of twenty members. The constitution provides that, when demanded, the vote must be by sections and that any one section may veto the work of the other two, but this provision has never yet been used and the committee acts as one body. An effort was made on the floor of the International Sunday-School Convention in 1914 to instruct its section of the Lesson Committee to stand for maintaining a uniform lesson in some form, but the attempt failed. The sessions of the committee have been characterized by many differences of opinion but by great brotherliness and complete harmony in final recommendations.

Denominational agencies quicken interest in religious education.—The new Lesson Committee pointed to a day when the Sunday-school agencies should once more be under one common leadership to supervise the common elements of their programs. While families in this world are often selfish, and thus far have effectually blocked any large success in communism, they seem to be the most effective agencies for the nurture of the young that society knows. Denominations may be quite as selfish at times and perhaps not quite as necessary to society as the family, nevertheless it must be granted that they have been very effective units for Sunday-school promotion.

It cannot be denied that since the organization of strong, aggressive denominational agencies for the promotion of Sunday-school work, the interest in religious education has moved forward by leaps and bounds. However, there has been a need for one body to supervise the promotional elements which are common to all of the denominations as well as need for societies with influence and authority enough to reach the last individual church. The denominational organizations can do the latter, but an inter-denominational agency is required to do the former task.

Necessity for united effort and common supervision.—Sunday-school methods and materials were greatly improved between the years 1910 and 1920 while numerically the advance was far greater than in any other decade of American history. New movements, such as that for Daily Vacation Bible Schools and the Week-Day Church Schools, came into prominence. The necessity for common effort in the promotion of week-day church schools, as well as in the preparation of teacher-training materials and in the supervision of community training schools, became increasingly evident. Should the agency for common promotion be under the control of the denominations acting jointly, or be under a body independent of denominational control? The International Sunday-School Association and the World's Sunday-School Association prided themselves upon their independence, although in the nature of the case the members of their executive boards were practically all of them members of some denomination. On the other hand, the denominations were just beginning to recognize the possibilities of religious education in the local church as well as the necessity for it, and had no notion of committing this promotion to agencies entirely independent of their control.

Reorganization begun.—The World's Sunday-School Association reorganized its Executive Committee in 1916 so as to give the denominations representation to the extent of fifty per cent of its members. However, there were still many who believed that the International should remain independent. In 1918 it was evident that either the Sunday-School Council, hitherto an advisory body only, must enlarge its scope and build up an organization to do executive work or else the International Sunday-School Association must reorganize itself so as to be officially the representative of the denominations. For several years these two bodies had maintained a Joint Committee on Standards. Each had also maintained a Committee on Reference and Counsel which had held numerous conferences together. Through these and other means, both organizations had begun to understand each other more perfectly. In 1918 each body named its own Committee on Reference and Counsel to represent it on a joint committee to bring about a reorganization of both agencies with the view of uniting upon a common program.

In 1920 a plan for reorganization was effected in the annual meetings of the executive bodies of each organization. This plan provided that fifty per cent of the members of the Executive Committee of the International Sunday-School Association should be territorial representatives, selected as formerly to represent the International Sunday-School Convention and the territorial, State, and Provincial Associations, while fifty per cent should be selected as official representatives of the cooperating denominations. It was also provided that the full-time paid workers of the International Sunday-School Association and its auxiliaries should be admitted to the membership of the Sunday-School Council of Evangelical Denominations.

However, it is one thing to perfect an organization upon paper and quite a different thing to carry it out. In June, 1920, both the Executive Committee of the International Sunday-School Association and the Sunday-School Council met on the same days and in the same place, Buffalo, New York, to welcome the new members in each group. In January and February, 1921, the reorganized Council and the reorganized Executive Committee of the International held their annual meetings. It was decided here that two steps were necessary to move toward the complete union of the two bodies; first that the auxiliary associations in the States must be helped to reorganize and then to develop a program in common with the denominations, and, second, that one common Committee on Education should be created. This committee was duly constituted, assigned supervision over all educational matters, and asked to report for approval to the two bodies creating them.

This Committee on Education is composed of representative Sunday-school officials of the denominations and of the International Association with its auxiliaries, professors of religious education and Bible, experts in the field of general education, and public-school leaders. The committee held its first meeting on April 26, 27, 28, in Buffalo and organized as follows: *Chairman*, Walter S. Athearn; *Vice-Chairman*, F. Carl Eiselen;

Secretary, George Platt Knox; *Treasurer,* Rufus W. Miller; *Chairmen of Standing Sub-Committees:* Luther A. Weigle, W. W. Charters, W. E. Raffety, Wade Crawford Barclay, John W. Shackford. The work of the new Committee on Education is in its beginnings, and the two organizations which created the Committee are in process of amalgamation, but it is the belief of those who are close to the developments that the forces of religious education, united as never before, will soon be able to give America the constructive leadership in this field so greatly needed.

Complete merger.—The most recent chapter in the history of these two international agencies for Sunday-school promotion begins with the action taken in Chicago in February, 1922, at the meeting of the Sunday-School Council of Evangelical Denominations. Here the Joint Committee on Reference and Counsel, which had often been given the task of reconciling differences between the two organizations, presented the following resolutions, which were unanimously adopted:

1. The reorganized Executive Committee of the International Sunday-School Association, based on the agreement of cooperation and Exhibit "A" (January-February, 1920) is the merged body of Territorial and Denominational forces as formerly represented by the International Sunday-School Association and the Sunday-School Council of Evangelical Denominations.

2. This merged body shall be called The International Sunday-School Council of Religious Education.

3. The International Sunday-School Council of Religious Education shall appoint a Committee on Education composed of not more than sixty members.

4. The International Sunday-School Council of Religious Education shall set up groups of professional workers, the Chairman of each of which shall be a con-

sulting member of the International Sunday-School Council of Religious Education.

These groups shall be such as Children's Workers, Young People's Workers, Adult Workers, Field Workers, Directors of Religious Education, Denominational Editors, Denominaticnal Publishers, etc.

5. We recommend that the Executive Committee of the Sunday-School Association request the Congress of the United States to amend the Charter by changing the name "The International Sunday-School Association," to "The International Sunday-School Council of Religious Education."

6. Pending the change of the legal name of the organization by Congressional action, we recommend that the business of the organization shall be conducted under the new name.

7. We recommend that the International Executive Committee be requested to revise its By-Laws in harmony with the foregoing provisions.

The Executive Committee of the International Sunday-School Association, which was legally the International Sunday-School Association, adopted the same recommendations at its meeting in Chicago, February 14, 15, 1922, and as soon as details can be perfected, there will be just one new organization—The International Sunday-School Council of Religious Education, performing its functions through conventions, special conference groups, an Education Committee of "not more than sixty," and an executive body which represents officially all of the cooperating denominations as well as all of the cooperating territorial units. The Sixteenth International Sunday-School Convention approved the action of the Executive Committee on June 22, 1922, in Kansas City, Missouri. It is expected that the State and Provincial Associations as they now exist will modify their form of organization so as to become auxiliary to the new body.

Achievements of the Sunday-School Council.— The principal services rendered to the cause of religious education by the Sunday-School Council of Evangelical Denominations, which merged itself into the new International Sunday-School Council of Religious Education after a career of twelve years, are the following:

1. The bringing about of a fairly clear understanding of their aims between many denominations and of how far in religious education they can act together in working out a common program for the nations involved.

2. The development of mutual understanding and close friendship on the part of denominational Sunday-school leaders who represent communions of widely differing viewpoints in theology and in organization for religious work.

3. The stimulation to greater creative activity in religious education through the association of small groups of denominational specialists who work in the same field.

4. Marked achievement in assisting to create and promote a system of International Graded Lessons and other improvements in curriculum materials.

5. The creation of the present standards of teacher training in the local church.

6. The creation of higher standards for all departments of Sunday-school activity in the local church.

These achievements are not claimed as exclusively to the credit of the Sunday-School Council of Evangelical Denominations, for International Association workers rendered great assistance both in the creation and also in the promotion of higher standards and better materials. But the denominational workers when once organized felt that the initiating of plans for religious education in the local church belonged to them, and they exercised this prerogative with painstaking and often sacrificial diligence.

Achievements of the International Sunday-School Association.—So much detail concerning the activities of this Association has been given that a summary of achievements is unnecessary. From 1872 to 1910 it was clearly in the ascendancy as a leader, the denominations gladly working through this organization and its auxiliaries although not officially related to it. When the great rise of denominational interest came, the Association was handicapped by some inevitable misunderstandings and conflicts over prerogatives. But the record of the Association leaders for painstaking effort to find the right road to more perfect service, in addition to their record for leading and assisting in creative as well as promotional work, is above reproach. They wielded power helpfully when it was undisputed, and they took in their officially appointed denominational partners most graciously when that action seemed to be wise. Both groups of workers were honestly seeking to find the best means of assisting the child, the youth, and the adult to realize his highest possibilities as a citizen of the kingdom (or family) of God.

SUMMARY

We have noted in this chapter the rise and developments of the agencies which have been most conspicuous in promoting religious education for Protestant children in the United States. We have not listed all of the organizations because we desired to concentrate attention upon a few. Each of the agencies noted has played a very powerful and helpful role in the development of Christian citizens in this land and abroad. What the future may hold for any one of them is uncertain. . They have made a new day of educational advance possible. It is to be hoped that each one will find its place in the new movements and continue to render highly effective service.

Topics for discussion:

1. Are national organizations necessary for the promotion of religious education in the United States?

2. Why were the churches, most of them, so slow to assume responsibility for the promotion of the modern Sunday school?

3. Investigate and compare the missionary work of the American Sunday-School Union for the first quarter century of its history with its missionary work for the last quarter of a century.

4. What kind of reading material did the American Sunday-School Union send out in the first half of the nineteenth century? Estimate its value in that pioneer day.

5. Is the big Sunday-school convention as popular and helpful to-day as it was in the last half of the nineteenth century?

6. What are the most important contributions made by the International Sunday-School Association to the cause of religious education?

7. To what extent is a World's Sunday-School Association needed? What are the greatest accomplishments of this association? What are its plans for development in the next few years?

8. In what ways does the Religious Education Association serve most effectively to-day?

9. Explain the rise of denominational agencies for Sunday-school promotion.

10. Would you have voted for the reorganization of the International Sunday-School Association and of the Sunday-School Council of Evangelical Denominations looking toward a complete merger of the two bodies?

11. How much can a national Committee on Education as created by the International Sunday-School Council of Religious Education reasonably be expected to accomplish in the next ten years?

Brief bibliography of selected references:

Rice—*The Sunday-School Movement and the American Sunday-School Union, 1817–1917.* The American Sunday-School Union, 1917.

Organized Sunday-School Work in America, 1908–1911: Official Report of the Thirteenth International Sunday-School Convention, San Francisco, California, 1911.

Official Reports:
International Sunday-School Conventions.
World's Sunday-School Association Conventions.
State Sunday-School Conventions.
Religious Education Association Conventions.
Minutes of the Annual Meetings of the Sunday-School Council of Evangelical Denominations.
Denominational Boards of Sunday Schools.
Denominational editors.

Encyclopedia of Sunday-Schools and Religious Education. Vols. I–III. Thos. Nelson and Sons, New York, 1915.

Periodicals:
    The Church School.
    Religious Education.
    The Sunday-School Times.
Leaflets prepared by Sunday-School Associations and
    Denominational Boards of Sunday Schools or
    Boards of Religious Education.

CHAPTER VIII

BEGINNINGS OF WEEK-DAY RELIGIOUS INSTRUCTION

FOR many years Christian workers have tried to solve the problem of how to get more time for religious instruction than one hour on Sunday. Ideally religious education and general education should not be separated. Religious education provides the motives, and some of the information which the teacher of public education most needs if he is to develop in young lives the attitudes of reverence for sacred things, of appreciation for beauty in form and conduct, and of a desire to help one's comrades.

If the term "education" comprehends the whole process of nurturing a life, and if such nurture involves the development of right attitudes as well as the acquiring of useful information, and the cultivation of skills, then clearly the development of God-consciousness and an increasing ability to do God's will cannot properly be left out of the educational system of a Christian nation.

Few in America desire that it should be left out. Even those whose theories of a mechanical development of all the faculties see no place for a personal God in the process, recognize that it is difficult to produce a socially minded citizen without giving him some motive for his conduct higher than that of pure selfishness. They also recognize that, historically, faith in God has supplied this adequate motive in the minds of many people. It is reasonable to suppose that even the non-Christian educator would be glad to see some form of instruction which would stimulate the growth of a moral dynamic equivalent to Christian faith.

DIFFICULTIES INHERENT IN PUBLIC-SCHOOL SYSTEM

The trouble, of course, lies in the fact that religion being one's conception of the highest good in life, it is impossible to secure agreement as to what kind of religion shall be taught in a nation composed of people from all quarters of the globe. In the early days of America, when communities were homogeneous racially and religiously, the problem was simple. Religious materials were used as a means in general education. In mission lands the Christian boarding schools and day schools may do the same to-day unless there is vigorous opposition from some quarter, but in the average American community it is impossible.

This nation with its ideals of democracy could not commit the power of government to ignorant people, nor could it rely upon individual churches, rich and poor, to educate their own constituencies as their desires and resources might permit. A democracy must not only have an intelligent citizenry, but it must have a citizenry with common ideals, with love for each other and for country, with ability to do their full share toward helping the nation to realize its common ideals.

It was with reluctance that the Christians of any church gave up control over the general education of their children. Those who did this willingly did so because they realized that there was no other way to guarantee the development of a great free republic. Other churches insisted upon withholding cooperation from the public schools. Out of sheer necessity, the churches of America were compelled to find some way of giving religion its rightful place in the development of child life. Thus far since the complete separation between State education and religious education, the Sunday school has been the most outstanding teaching institution through which the church has tried to instruct all of the people.

Time schedules.—In the schools of Robert Raikes, the Sunday school had five hours on the Lord's Day. In the Sunday schools promoted in America by the Methodist Episcopal Church the time schedule was "from six o'clock in the morning until ten; and from two o'clock in the afternoon till six, when it does not interfere with public worship."[1]

In colonial days we find on Sunday frequently a preaching service in the morning and a teaching service in the afternoon.

However, by 1840 it was common to give the Sunday school not more than an hour and a half, while to-day, very many schools have only one hour for worship, instruction, and expression combined.

Since 1900 many experiments have been undertaken in order to secure more time for religious instruction and to secure some kind of correlation with the public school. In New York city some years ago the clergy, including Protestants, Catholics, and Jews, tried to agree to request the public-school authorities to dismiss the pupils early on a particular afternoon so that they could go to their churches for religious instruction. In fact, for years the Catholics and Jews have had public-school children go to their church schools for religious instruction after public school hours. Such a

---

[1] Wardle—*History of the Sunday-School Movement in the Methodist Episcopal Church*, p. 52. Methodist Book Concern, New York, 1918. Used by permission.

plan might have become general fifteen years ago if the Protestant churches had possessed the necessary teaching force and equipment to care for the pupils.

Another experiment which was receiving considerable attention in 1910 to 1914 was the combined preaching-teaching service. In this the pupils went directly to their departments and classes for study, then into the service of public worship, and then back to class. Or there might be two periods of class work before the service of public worship.

A few churches may still be following such a plan, but most of those that made the experiment have abandoned the scheme. The agencies for the promotion of religious education are not promoting this combined service for the simple reason that they believe that there are better methods of securing additional time.

Daily Vacation Bible Schools.—Approximately twenty years ago Robert G. Boville, in New York city (1901), and H. R. Vaughn, in Truax Prairie, Wisconsin (1900), inaugurated types of Vacation Bible Schools. The plans were similar in principle but different in important details. The underlying principle was to use vacation time for a period of from ten days to six weeks for school work in the field of religious instruction. Bible stories were given a prominent place in the curriculum and in order to emphasize the play element, music, hammock weaving or sewing, and other expressional forms of work received a relatively large amount of attention in the schools of the East. The average term in the East was five weeks; in the West the schools were usually of short duration and practically eliminated all activities which did not have a decided bearing on Bible instruction.

The Federal Council of Churches of New York promoted these schools at first under the supervision of the Baptist City Missionary Society. Later the Presbyterian, Methodist, and other denominations put their promotion agencies back of the movement.

In 1911 the movement under the leadership of Dr. Boville was incorporated as the International Association of Daily Vacation Bible Schools, and in 1921 this Association was reorganized so as to give the denominations official representation on the Board of Directors. How rapidly the movement has spread may be noted by the fact that in 1911 the Association reported 102 schools, 509 teachers, and 26,886 pupils, with an estimated expenditure of $26,578.99. The work was then confined principally to four cities of the East. But by 1921 the movement had spread into many communities all over the country, and the Association reported 2,534 schools, 15,555 teachers, and 270,000 children with an estimated expenditure of $270,000.

Typical schedule.—The following is a typical school schedule as given in a bulletin of the Association (1922 edition) entitled "Facts for all Lovers of Little Children":

THE SCHEDULE

FIRST PERIOD

8:30—Preparation and visitation by staff.

9:00—Doors open and registration.

SECOND PERIOD

9:15—Opening worship, all present.
Hymn.
Psalm or other portion, repeated in concert.

Lord's Prayer—repeated or sung.
Kindergarten goes out.
Health, Habit or Patriotic Talk.
Thank-offering for Extension.
Bible Memory Work.

9:40—Musical Period.
Vocal and breathing exercises.

Singing lesson.
Calisthenics with music.

10:05—Bible lessons.
　Told as story by the
　teacher, or
　Represented by children,
　or
　Taught with sand table, or
　Given with stereopticon.

THIRD PERIOD

10:30—Expressional Activities.
　Simple dramatization of
　Bible stories.
　Manual work and play
　in sections.
　H a m m o c k-m a k i n g,
　Weaving.
　Raffia work, Basketry,
　Sewing.
　Bible Hand Work.

Doing something for
others, such as Red
Cross work.
Work for Children's Hos-
pitals.
First Aid and Hygiene.

11:25—Closing exercises—School
re-assembles.
Daily salute to flags.
See order in manual.
"America" or Hymn.
Children's Benediction.
Recessional March.

AFTERNOON—TWO HOURS

2:30—Open air games organized
and directed.
Excursions.
Visitation of homes.
Weekly Conference, Mon-
day.
Mother's Meetings.

The Vaughn type.—Dr. Vaughn has never organized an association for the promotion of the schools that follow his plans, but the work in Wisconsin has developed conspicuously under his leadership, and some of the leading denominations are inclined to favor his emphasis upon religious instruction to the exclusion of some of the recreational features used in the East. *The Vacation Religious Day School*, written by Hazel Straight Stafford, who for several years taught in schools under Dr. Vaughn's supervision, indicates clearly the curriculum material and general plans used in the Vaughn type of school.

Growing movement.—The movement is growing rapidly, and has already made a substantial contribution to general interest and specific technique in religious education. Its program is much easier to carry out than that of the week-day church school, but it seems reasonable to suppose that within the next few years it will become an integral part of an all-the-year week-day church-school program, and will likewise be correlated with the Sunday program of the church school.

EXPERIMENTS OF WEEK-DAY INSTRUCTION

Several significant experiments in week-day religious education have been made.

North Dakota plan for high school credit.—In 1911 Sunday-school workers were thrilled by the announcement of the North Dakota Plan for High School Credit in Bible Study. Through the influence of Vernon P. Squires, a professor in the University of North Dakota, the State Board of Education prepared a syllabus and authorized that a certain limited amount of high-school credit (one-half unit) should be given to any one passing an examination on the historical and literary facts of the Bible indicated in the syllabus.[2] The work could be taken in the Sunday school or outside of it under carefully defined conditions, and credit would be awarded upon the passing of an examination conducted by the State.

This seemed to the Sunday-school workers to be clear proof that the States were beginning to recognize not only the importance of biblical and other religious training, but the ability of the Sunday school to teach the necessary religious materials. It also pointed out a way in which church and state might cooperate in school work without encroaching upon the rights of each other. Thus far no serious difficulty in the administration of the plan has arisen.

---

[2] Wood—*School and College Credit for Outside Bible Study*, pp. 66ff.

Professor Squires and his helpers deserve great credit as pioneers. The scheme in itself was not so significant as some supposed, but it was a beginning along the right line and started many people to thinking, trying to invent new plans.

Colorado plan.—In September, 1910, Dr. D. D. Forward,[3] a Baptist pastor in Greeley, Colorado, suggested to the authorities of the State Teachers College, located in that city, that if they would credit his work he would teach a class in Bible in his own church. The plan was accepted and in September, 1911, two hundred and fifty students elected the course of Bible Study on Jesus, sixty of this number being members of the Roman Catholic Church.[4] The popularity of the plan led to its extension so as to include high-school credit, and a committee was appointed through the influence of Colorado Sunday-School Association to standardize the requirements for giving high-school credit to Bible study taken in the Sunday school. Catholics and Protestants united in formulating the standards, and many classes began to take work for credit. This experiment aroused great interest in some Sunday-school circles. The International Sunday-School Association created a commission to investigate and promote this work, while several State Associations appointed committees to try to put either the Colorado plan or a modification of it into operation immediately in their States. Indiana, Kansas, and Washington did start such a movement, but the commission of the International made little headway and finally disbanded.

Two features worked against the success of the plan.

---

[3] *Teacher's Handbook of the Colorado Plan of Bible Study for Colleges and High Schools,* p. 3. Printed by The State Sunday-School Association of Colorado.

[4] Wood—*School and College Credit for Outside Bible Study,* pp. 43, 66ff.

In the first place, as the writer pointed out in the commission, the plan provided for credit in Bible study only, whereas most of the leading denominations had introduced considerable extra-biblical material into their regular Sunday-school curricula for high-school students. In the International Graded Lessons as used by these denominations the pupils with ages from fourteen to seventeen inclusive, grades 9, 10, 11, and 12 of the high school, were studying not only Bible heroes with especial emphasis upon the life of Jesus, but also church history heroes, heroes of modern missions, church administration, and vocational problems. In order to cooperate with the proposed movement for high-school credit, these churches would have been required to displace all of their extra-biblical material in favor of courses in biblical literature and history.

Since they had but recently won the battle for a more practical curriculum and were beginning to get gratifying results in improved Bible study and improved service ability with their new materials, they had no notion of going backward in this matter for the sake of high-school credit. If the plan had involved credit for "religious instruction," defining simply the academic conditions under which the work should be done and leaving to each church the privilege of determining for itself the content of religious instruction, it would have enlisted much greater support than it received.

Again, the movement was handicapped because some saw in it a "short cut" to successful religious education. They expected the allurement of credit to win to the Sunday-school young people who were then out of the school because the teachers were too incompetent to hold them. A man was speaking to the writer enthusiastically about the possibilities of high-school credit in his city. Since a recent convention had inspired him with the notion the writer attempted to show how he could put his own school in readiness to do creditable work when the Board of Education should act favorably. He pointed out that steps must be taken to train the teachers, to improve the organization of the school, and to improve the curriculum. "But," exclaimed the man, impatiently, "I am not interested in improving this school, I am interested in high-school credit." "Then, my friend," came the reply, "you are interested in the least important phase of the whole question. If the Board of Education of your city should determine to-night that credit might be awarded under certain conditions, not six Sunday schools in this great city could qualify as they are running at present, and certainly yours could not."

There was also considerable discussion in the commission about legal difficulties in certain States, but the movement was dropped at the time, 1916, for lack of interest and not because of legal difficulties. Nevertheless, the question of high-school credit for "religious instruction" under proper conditions is a very live question at present, and the North Central Association of Colleges and Secondary Schools recently appointed a committee to define a unit in religious instruction and the academic conditions under which extra-mural credit in this field may be granted. When this has been done the Sunday schools, by improving their teaching force and their classroom conditions, while using the proper units of their regular curricula, will be awarded credit, and this form of cooperation between church schools and public schools will be upon a firm foundation.

The Gary Church Schools.—Another experiment in the effort to secure additional time for religious instruction began in Gary, Indiana, late in the year of 1913. Indiana, through the leadership of the State Sunday-School Association, had already worked out a plan for high-school credit modeled somewhat after the Colorado Plan, so that cooperation between the church and the public school was not an untried thing in this State. However, the Gary experiment arose through none of the plans previously mentioned, but because of the unique character of the Gary public schools carrying out the theories of William Wirt, their superintendent.

Professor Wirt is a thoroughgoing believer in the unity of the educational process. He believes that a good school should guide a student in the use of his leisure and in his occupational desires as well as in his study. Hence he calls his schools "Work, Study, Play Schools." He believes in a longer school day in order to guide the use of more of the pupil's time. The Gary school day is from 8 A. M. to 5 P. M. with night classes for those who desire them. He also believes in religious education as an important factor in the development of any child, and holds that the lengthened school day should provide a place for religion as it does for play, for music, and other useful activities. In order to get the maximum use out of the Gary buildings he organized his school system so that "A" school assembles at 8 A. M., and uses the recitation rooms for an hour, then goes to the playground and rooms devoted to expressional activities, while the "B" school assembles in the classrooms. Thus classrooms and expressional facilities are used constantly, and during the school day the pupil has time for religious as well as other studies if he so desires.

In the fall of 1913 Professor Wirt spoke to J. M. Avann, pastor of the Methodist Episcopal Church, and offered to release pupils to the churches for religious instruction if the pastors cared to avail themselves of this offer. Dr. Avann at once called the pastors together, and they accepted this opportunity promptly. Not having the funds necessary to finance the new project, some of these churches through their pastors appealed to the boards in charge of promoting religious education in their respective denominations. The Baptist, Congregational, Disciples of Christ, Methodist Episcopal, Presbyterian, and Protestant Episcopal Boards all responded with some help, and week-day schools of religion were begun by some of the churches in the fall of 1914.

· In the fall of 1915 the following directors were giving full time to the organization of week-day schools in their churches:

Myron C. Settle, Disciples of Christ.

Harry Webb Farrington, Methodist.

Thomas Owens, Presbyterian.

Miss Vera L. Noyes, Protestant Episcopal.

The Baptist Church, under the leadership of H. E. Wilson, pastor, conducted a school using local people as teachers for fifty cents an hour and securing very great assistance from Selden L. Roberts, State superintendent of religious education of the Baptist denomination for Indiana.

In addition to those mentioned, schools were opened under the leadership of the pastor of the Congregational Church, while union classes were conducted in Neighborhood House and in Friendly House. The Jews conducted two schools, but made only slight use of the special schedule. The Roman Catholics did not open any special schools, since they already had strong parochial schools in the city.

The following table will give the enrollment of the schools in December, 1915, and other interesting information:[5]

Denomination	Pupils	Teacher's Salary	General Expenses First Year	Probably Second Year
Baptist	66	50c. per hour. Total last year, $250	Very Little	
Congregational	36	None	None except heat, $10	
Disciples of Christ	151	$1,800	$300	$150
Methodist Episcopal	111	1,800	250	150
Presbyterian	104	1,200 and $7 per month for house rent	62	50
Protestant Episcopal	59	750	250	150
Jewish (Orthodox)	56	1,800 (all expenses)		
Jewish (Reformed)	36	None	None	

From the beginning the church schools were successful in holding the loyalty of pupils and parents. Although the teaching accommodations were inadequate and the curriculum material was far from satisfactory, Professor Wirt and others testified in 1915 that the plan had made religion a subject of conversation along with other topics of the school child, and that the conduct of the church-school children was abundant evidence that the schools were helping to develop Christian character.

The great forward step in the Gary Church Schools came in 1918, when five Protestant denominations united to form a community Board of Education and to create a community system of church schools.[6]

This made possible far more effective work at greatly reduced expenditures. It also enabled these churches to have schools near the public-school buildings, whereas under the old plan most of the church-school classes

---

[5] *Religious Education*, February, 1916, p. 6. From article entitled "The Week-Day Church Schools of Indiana," a report of an investigation by Arlo A. Brown.

[6] *Week-Day Religious Instruction as Conducted at Gary*, copyright 1921, William Grant Seaman, Mary Elizabeth Abernethy.

were held in the churches located near the Jefferson
School, which was not even the "Central School" of
the city. In the new system where churches were not
conveniently located, special "huts" (similar to those
used in war work) were built, and in one case in 1920,
while waiting for the erection of a building, the public-
school property itself was used.

Since the beginning of the community system the
teaching force has been under the able supervision of
a principal, Miss Mary Elizabeth Abernethy, and a
competent corps of instructors has been developed.
The statistics will tell their story concerning the growth
of these schools.

COMMUNITY WEEK-DAY CHURCH SCHOOLS OF GARY

Year	No. Schools Operated	No. of Teaching Staff	Initial Enrollment	Total Enrollment
1917-18.....	3	Principal and three teachers	450	800
1918-19.....	7	Principal and five teachers	800	2,100
1919-20.....	8	Principal and five teachers (plus three part time teachers)	1,600	3,100
1920-21.....	8	Principal and seven teachers	2,400	3,700
1921-22.....	8	Principal and six teachers	2,900	*3,100

* Decrease due, first, to financial depression, causing reduction of the teaching staff, and also causing families to withdraw their children when they could
not contribute; due, secondly, to the organization of other church schools outside of this system.

**Significance of the Gary-school plan and Gary-
church-school plan.**—Many have thought that the
significance of the Gary Church Schools is lessened by
the fact that they are involved in the Gary Public-
School Plan. The position is erroneous. The Gary
Public-School System does give the Gary Church
Schools some advantages and it also gives them some
handicaps. But the sympathetic insight of Professor
Wirt, and the educational principles which he has
popularized in the community are the chief advantages.
If a school system is to guide in work, study, and play,

the elimination of religion from a place in that program would seem to be unthinkable. Furthermore, the writer ventures the opinion that, quite apart from any consideration of the Gary public-school time schedule, Professor Wirt is absolutely right in insisting that the school should guide a larger portion of the pupil's life and that religious instruction is a necessary feature in such guidance.

The chief significance, then, of the Gary School Plan to religious education is that it recognized the importance of religious instruction and offered to the churches an opportunity to provide such during school hours when the pupil was unfatigued. This applied, however, only to children whose parents desired it. It gave the churches an opportunity which they accepted, and the publicity given to the peculiar features of the Gary Public Schools likewise gave the church-school movement great publicity. For eight years the Gary Week-Day Church Schools have been conducted successfully. Their workers did not seek the publicity which came to them, and in a sense it was a handicap to be thus "set on a hill," but they have steadily improved their work, and to-day these schools are far more effective and more firmly established in the affections of the Gary people than ever before. The church-school leaders in Gary have given to the world a good object lesson, and they expect other schools to improve on their materials and methods.

As previously indicated, the idea of taking children into the church for instruction after school hours was not new in 1914. The Jewish religious leaders have long conducted successful schools at such a time, but the idea of getting public-school children dismissed from classes during school hours in order to attend a church school for religious instruction was practically new. Although there were isolated cases of this, such as the Wenner plan in New York, the idea did not receive widespread attention until tried out in Gary. To-day, however, Gary is only one of the communities in which week-day church schools are flourishing.

In Hammond, Whiting, and Indiana Harbor, nearby cities, in 1922, there were 3,200 pupils enrolled in the week-day classes even though the Gary public-school schedule is not in operation. In these three cities, having a common director of religious education, there are ninety-two teachers employed on part time and one teacher on full time.

The Van Wert plan.—One of the most significant experiments is in Van Wert (Ohio), whose church-school system is patterned after the Gary Church-School System, and uses the same curriculum. However, Van Wert has made no small contribution to the movement by working out the details of such a school so that it can be made to fit a rural community. Let us quote from the description of the school as given by the Van Wert workers themselves:[7]

"In this plan no pretence is made to originality. In the main it follows the Gary Plan, although in adapting the work to the ordinary public-school system, and by using the school time for classes, Van Wert has placed the work on a basis that is feasible for the average community, and so economical that smaller communities may dare to venture in a like experiment. The success of the third year in Van Wert warrants the passing on of the main features of the plan to others who are looking for help. The simplicity of the Van

---

[7] *Van Wert Plan of Week-Day Religious Instruction,* Mary K. Cowles. Ernest I. Antrim, p. 2, The Pioneer Press, Van Wert, Ohio, 1921. Used by permission.

Wert plan is one of its strong characteristics. A large city might find it difficult to get the cooperation of the public school for an all-day schedule for classes, but Van Wert school authorities and citizens sensed the value of the work at the start, and were willing to arrange for a continuous schedule of classes for the Bible teacher like that of the music and art teacher. This allows a trained teacher to use her full time in the work, thus giving greater unity to the instruction and requiring a minimum of supervision. Moreover, it reduces the liability of poor teaching which may result when many teachers are employed. There is also an economic advantage, because the equipment provided for the classes may be used all day, and the expenditure for heat and janitor service may be kept at the lowest possible figure."[8]

The Batavia plan.—Another modification of the plan is found in Batavia, Illinois, where every Thursday throughout the school year the children of the eight grades go to their respective churches for one hour or more of religious instruction. By united action of all the churches, brought about through the ministerial association, the school board readily granted the request. The children come in successive groups of two and three grades at a time. The system was established in 1919. Mr. Hoag makes the following significant statement.

"In some forty weeks of operation there has not been reported a single case of truancy. This means that the children like the work. If a child comes to public school on Thursday, he also comes to his church school. Can

---

[8] It should be noted that only a small percentage of the population of Van Wert is Roman Catholic, hence the free use of public-school buildings does not involve difficulties which might attend such use elsewhere.

any Sunday school boast of such a record—of having no absences except for physical causes? Tardiness has been negligible. There are seven hundred and twenty-five children of the eight grades in Batavia, and of these all but fifteen now have chosen some church and receive religious instruction on Thursdays. This was not true at the start, but by careful explaining, calling, and checking of lists, we have reached this remarkable showing. This means that over ninety-seven per cent of the children in the grades are receiving the instruction. One hour a week for eight years—and this for every child in town—is a prospect that must appeal to every religious institution. With such a system permanent, the effect on the young people of a town is bound to be toward the making of more numerous and more faithful church members."[9]

Utah plan of religious education for high-school students.—Another very significant type of week-day church school is that begun by the Church of Jesus Christ of Latter-Day Saints. In 1912, just across from the Granite High School, in Salt Lake County, was erected a small building, since called a seminary, with one good classroom, a principal's office, and an entrance hall. In this institution the students of the high school registered for courses in the Bible. To-day there are twenty-seven such seminaries adjacent to public high schools, with a total enrollment of 3,400. The course of study covered to date comprises three years of work: 1. Old Testament Studies; 2. New Testament Studies; 3. Church History and Doctrine. The last named is strictly sectarian and carries no credit.

Of this plan Adam S. Bennion, superintendent of the

---

[9] See "Week-Day Religious Instruction in Batavia, Ill.," by V. Hoag, *Religious Education*, December, 1920, p. 307ff.

Commission of Education of the Church of Latter Day Saints, Salt Lake City, says:

"As to the actual accomplishment of the seminary, the volume of commendatory statements of public high-school principals who have observed the work as it is done, of students who have taken the courses offered, and of parents of these students, indicate that this institution is one of the greatest forces for righteousness ever operated by the Church of Jesus Christ of Latter-Day Saints. It makes it possible for a church to sustain the public school as the one great guarantee of American democracy and still gives to the youth of our land that sense of their relationship to God which anchors them to the faith of those great men and women who founded that Democracy. It makes possible the achievement of the ideal expressed by Professor Athearn in this memorable statement, 'The world will never be safe for Democracy until intelligence and godliness are the common possession of the whole human family.' "[10]

A SURVEY OF THE RELIGIOUS EDUCATION ASSOCIATION

Other schools which the student can very profitably study are those in Toledo, Ohio; Evanston, Illinois; Oak Park, Illinois; Cuyahoga Falls, Ohio; New York City; and Malden, Mass. All of these represent successful experiments with significant variations in organization, curricula, and other features. A very valuable study of the whole movement has recently been made by the Religious Education Association with the cooperation of the Committee on Social and Religious Surveys, a Continuation Committee of the Interchurch World Movement. The Association devoted practically

---

[10] *Religious Education*, February 1922, p. 54.

the entire program of its annual convention in Chicago, March 29–April 1, 1922, to the subject of week-day church schools. In preparation for this discussion the facts concerning the present situation in the schools now being conducted were secured by Edwin L. Shaver, at that time professor of religious education, Hendrix College. His survey sets forth the facts so far as they could be ascertained statistically and supplemented by personal observation in many typical schools. It will reward the most careful study.[11]

According to this survey, there were in the United States at the time the survey was made 324 week-day church schools of the general type under discussion, not including vacation Bible schools, parochial schools, or Jewish schools. Of these, 155 were single schools operating independently, while 169 operated in 44 community systems. Three hundred of these schools reported a total enrollment of 15,536 boys and 16,592 girls. Mr. Shaver estimates the total enrollment for all of the schools at about 50,000. He classified the schools according to four types:

Type 1. The denominational or individual church type.

Type 2. The denominational-cooperating type (loose federation).

Type 3. The neighborhood or city system (where schools lose their denominational character and merge their interests with others to provide a common course of study).

Type 4. The pure community type (in which the governing board does not represent the churches but the community at large).

---

[11] *Religious Education*, April, p. 83ff.

No school of Type 4 was known to the surveyor when the report was prepared, although a few had started as such and changed to Type 3. He found the prevailing types to be as follows: Total single schools (Types 1 and 2), 155; Total schools in a system according to Type 3, 169; total, 324.

Legal aspects.—Of especial interest to many are the legal phases of this new type of school. Charles L. Dibble, in his paper on "Specific Legal Provisions in Week-Day School,"[12] makes the following convenient classification:

Type A. A room is set apart in the public-school building, to which any denomination is at liberty to send a teacher for religious instruction during school hours. Children whose parents so request are sent to this room from their classrooms at the time assigned to their denomination.

Type B. Courses in religious instruction are established by one or more denominations in their own church buildings at hours (during school hours) agreed upon; children whose parents so request are sent from their school buildings to these classes; the courses of instruction are more or less under the supervision of the public-school authorities and credit is given for work completed in the church school, and attendance enforced under the truancy law.

Type C. Same as Type B, except that the instruction is not in any way subject to the supervision of the public-school authorities and no credit is given. Attendance is not enforced under the truancy law. If, however, the child habitually absents himself from the church school, that fact is reported to the public school, and the privilege of attendance is withdrawn.

---

[12] *Religious Education*, pp. 42ff.

Of Type C he says:

This scheme contemplates a complete divorce of the church school from the public-school system. No credit is asked for work accomplished; and attendance is not enforced under the truancy law. If the child is habitually truant from the church school, he is simply reported to the public-school authorities and the privilege of attendance is withdrawn. The work of the church school is, then, in no sense a part of the school curriculum. In legal effect the child is excused from school in order to attend the church school on the ground that the absence is for his well-being and presents reasonable ground for that privilege. This plan presents none of the features which might in some jurisdictions, militate against the other two. It does not involve the use of a public building, or any expenditure of the time of the public-school teachers, nor does it make the religious instruction in any way a part of the public-school curriculum. It does, however, raise the question as to whether the compulsory school law authorizes the local authorities to permit the child to absent himself from school during school hours.[13]

Courses of study used.—While the curriculum for week-day church schools is uniquely in the experimental stage it will be of interest to mention some of the courses which are now being used. Professor Joseph M. Artman in an article entitled "An Evaluation of Curricula" describes briefly the following: Bible, Gary Leaflets, Abingdon Week-Day Series, Scribners, University of Chicago, Northwestern, Keystone, Lutheran, Christian Nurture, Roman Catholic, Catechism, other Sunday-school literature, Protestant Teachers' Association, Graded Bible Stories (Mutch), Toledo Course (Trettien), Lansing Syllabus, Oklahoma City Syllabus.[14]

[13] *Religious Education*, February, 1922, pp. 48ff.
[14] *Religious Education*, April, 1922, pp. 151ff.

Findings of the Convention of the Religious Education Association.—The convention will probably go down in history as one of the most largely attended and most influential in the history of the organization. A Committee on Findings presented an excellent summary of the prevailing opinions brought out in the discussions. Doubtless many in the convention would not accept this report as an expression of their own views, but it clearly expresses the highest educational ideals and attempts to impress upon all readers the necessity for proceeding slowly until an adequately trained leadership is ready to guide these week-day church schools.

The following is the report:[15]

The Nineteenth Annual Convention of the Religious Education Association is confronted by conditions which present, on the one hand, a challenge to greater achievement and, on the other, a ground for faith that this challenge will be met.

The challenge is found in conditions which compel our frank confession of failure thus far, with all that has been done in the name of religious education, to achieve a social experience worthy of religious ideals.

Our ground for faith is sound, first of all, in the face of this confession, for the first step toward improvement is in the recognition of the need.

Another ground of this faith is to be found in the marked increase of intelligent interest in the aims and methods of religious education manifested both by individuals and by organized groups.

A striking illustration of this interest is found in the development of and the widespread interest in the week-day school of religion which we have here discussed, an

---

[15] *Religious Education*, June, 1922, pp. 266ff.

interest further evidenced by the unexpectedly large and very representative attendance at this convention.

We recognize in this new movement what may prove to be a most effective agency in bringing about that improvement—the need of which we admit—provided that at its inception it has the guidance of a trained leadership moving toward carefully defined aims and taking advantage of the best that modern education has to offer.

This movement at present represents a fine expression of religious devotion with a recognition that something is wrong, or at least inadequate in our present programs of education. But there is also need of fearless self-examination and criticism. We must develop an educational conscience. We must recognize that with religious consecration there must be a consecration to educational science, and that joining these two we may hope to build a program of religious education worthy of our faith in God.

Aims

The aim of this movement is not mere instruction; it is not dogmatic nor ecclesiastical. We have as our goal the more and more adequate living of children in society, measured by the standards of religion.

Curriculum

It is plainly evident that the prevailing type of curriculum centers in biblical instruction. It is admitted, however, that the value of this instruction is to be tested by its results in experience. This conference has given evidence of a strong and growing consciousness that these values will be more adequately achieved by a curriculum which is organized about the experiences of children in society, and that this approach would also conserve the distinctive values of biblical instruction.

Organization

Each of the various types of organization now in use

has certain advantages. It is clearly evident that we have not yet reached the stage of development at which organization can be standardized. Indeed, it is doubtful if any one type of organization can be devised which will satisfactorily meet the needs of all communities. The ideal seems to be as close an approximation to the community type as the local conditions make advisable.

SUPERVISION

The problems of supervision in the school of religion are not essentially different from those in the general field of education. Skilled and effective supervision is absolutely essential. The function of the supervisor is to cooperate with teachers while they are working out their tasks in improving the quality of their teaching and in developing a more adequate religious educational experience for the children.

PUBLIC-SCHOOL RELATIONSHIPS

The week-day school is challenged by both the public school and the child to justify its claim for a share of their time and attention. School boards will not feel at liberty to grant a portion of that time of the pupil for which they are responsible unless they are assured that the experience of the pupil in the school of religion will measure up to public-school standards, nor will pupils give their attention to a program which does not awaken real interest. This is a legitimate challenge and one that the school of religion must frankly meet.

Provided this challenge is met, however, the school of religion is entitled to the opportunity to make its vital contribution to the education of the child. The importance of this contribution of the school of religion is as clearly and sympathetically recognized by the public-school men as by the church itself. The greatest hope of a satisfactory solution of these problems of relationship is found in this mutually sympathetic and cooperative attitude.

We affirm the principles stated in the resolutions of the Association at the conference of 1916:

"The church and state are to be regarded as distinct institutions, which, as far as possible, cooperate through the agency of their common constituents in their capacity as individual citizens.

"The work of religious instruction and training should be done by such institutions as the home, the church, and the private school, and not by the public school nor in official connection with the public school."

TEACHING METHODS

The problem-project type of teaching, rightly understood, involves purposeful participation by children in the educational process and making projects and problems growing out of the life of children and having religious significance the basis and center of the teaching. This is not so much a method as a point of view, and a point of view within which all valuable elements in the older approaches find their place. Teachers working from this approach can as readily grow into skill as under more traditional methods and its manifest superiority in the production of results leads us to recommend it as the general basis upon which the school of religion should be developed.

PREPARATION OF TEACHERS

It is apparent that high standards of professional training for teachers are a requisite for the success of week-day programs of religious education. Such programs may be postponed until teachers trained under such professional standards can be secured, or such professional training may be developed in part in experimental schools of religion where there is trained supervision.

Conclusion

Modern complex social conditions have raised a problem for the solution of which the religious education already developed is inadequate. Those interested in the progress of religion have been baffled by these conditions. The week-day religious school seems to give hope of realizing for the modern world a religious training more nearly adequate to meet present conditions. But the significance of the movement depends upon the trend of its development. If the week-day school simply gives more instruction of the type which modern education has rejected, the future of the movement is doomed. If it follows the trend which seems to represent the conviction of this convention and is embodied in these findings, we shall find in it a most significant agency of religious education.[16]

MOST DIFFICULT PROBLEMS

The two most difficult problems connected with the movement are (a) how to weld together the leading Protestant denominations of a community so as to create a community system of week-day church schools, and (b) how to relate the curriculum of the week-day church school to that of the Sunday school. The former problem is in process of solution. In many communities the difficulties will be slight; in others they will be insuperable until the individual churches by actual experience learn, as the people in Gary learned, that a common teaching staff for the community using a common curriculum and common equipment is far more efficient and far more economical than the plan of having each church conduct its own school.

The second problem would be easier to solve if there were not so many people in the Sunday schools of a

---

[16] Committee: Herbert W. Gates, J. W. F. Davies, Marie Cole Powell, William James Mutch, Harrison S. Elliot.

community who cannot possibly attend the week-day church schools, and if there were not different standards for the teachers of the two systems. The Sunday church school will probably for many years if not always make a large use of volunteer teachers, while the week-day church school, by practically common consent, seeks to secure paid teachers who are highly trained. Some publishers are preparing textbooks *de novo* for the week-day sessions without regard to the Sunday sessions, while the International Lesson Committee is trying to work out a unified curriculum for both week-day and Sunday sessions. Eventually the curriculum must be unified. The writer ventures the guess that it will contain the materials which the majority of cooperating churches believe should be used for the religious development of all the children in their respective communities. This will be the basic material and will be used on week days. Correlated with this will be the materials for Sunday sessions which will especially stress worship, together with the beliefs and activities of a particular denomination. In the high school and older groups probably separate short courses which are well correlated will be used.

Problems of leadership and finance.—In addition to the two most difficult problems, we should also mention the great problems of leadership and finance. The writer believes that there is an abundant supply of very promising leadership material eager to be trained for this service just as soon as these young people find that they will be able to support themselves in the new work. Creators of curriculum material and supervisors of teaching are the greatest needs of the hour in this phase of religious education. Those who are doing the best work are the most conscious of their limitations, and are increasing their ability steadily. In addition to these, new leaders with more adequate training are rapidly coming into the field. The suggestion that the churches should develop an order of professional teaching women for this work is worthy of complete support, and anyone who has interviewed many students of religious education cannot help but feel that there are many men as well as women who are eager to develop professionally in this field.

The problems of finance will usually be difficult wherever the churches do not cooperate. In a cooperative program the burden should not fall heavily upon any particular church. However, congregations which insist upon doing the work alone may find themselves handicapped for want of funds and equipment.

Bible teachers in public schools.—In a few communities such as Chattanooga, Tennessee, the Bible is being taught in public-school buildings like other regular subjects by teachers who are paid by the churches, but the plan has not been sufficiently tried to warrant the writer in hazarding a guess concerning the possibilities of such a plan in communities where the religious organizations represent very widely differing viewpoints.

SUMMARY

In previous chapters we noted how religious and general education were one process directed by one school system in the colonial period and in the early days of the new republic. Then we traced the process of separation until the public schools of the State had practically eliminated all definite religious instruction. In this chapter we have studied the developments toward giving religious education once more its proper amount of time and attention. We have noted the effort to lengthen the period for study on Sunday, the successful schools of religion conducted by the Jews and some individual churches after public school hours. Lastly we have discussed the rising movement for week-day schools of religion arranging their time schedules to fit into the schedules of the public school so that the pupil may have a chance to study religion when he is unfatigued.

It would be ridiculous to expect the perfection of such a system of schools overnight. The fact that the churches have supported eight years of experimentation with such schools before trying vigorously to propagate the plan is a good omen for its future success. Years will be required before the work can be done with maximum efficiency. But the principle upon which these schools are proceeding, the principle of cooperation between state and church schools with complete separation of administration, seems to be sound. No legal obstacles to the important features of the plan have yet appeared; and if the church schools are rightly conducted, they need not appear.

Such week-day church schools will not do away with the Sunday schools. Only the privileged ones who are in the public school can enjoy the advantages of the week-day church school, while practically every one not restrained by occupational duties can receive religious instruction on Sunday. Paid teachers are a necessity in the week-day schools, while literally millions of volunteer workers may be used successfully as officers and teachers in the Sunday school if the proper steps are taken to train and supervise these volunteers.

A sane and careful beginning has been made. Improvement of the materials and methods will be the task of the next few years, but there is every reason to expect a rapid development of this means of religious education. Colleges and graduate schools are already training the professional leadership. Just as soon as the churches are ready to put adequate financial resources at the disposal of these workers and to agree to promote in cooperation the common features of their greatest task, religious education, we may expect great success through this type of institution.

Questions for discussion:

1. Do you favor a public-school system if the elimination of religion from it is a necessity?
2. Is the elimination of direct Bible study and other religious materials from the public-school system of the United States a necessity?
3. Which of the plans for securing careful study of religious subjects on the part of public-school students do you consider the best?
4. Appraise the possible values of the Daily Vacation Bible School.
5. Appraise the significance of (a) the North Dakota Plan; (b) the Colorado Plan.
6. Describe a typical session in some grade of a week-day church school.
7. What is your estimate of the influence of the Gary Church Schools upon the promotion of week-day schools of religion?
8. Are the results of the week-day church schools up to date gratifying or disappointing?
9. Describe the principal types of week-day schools of religion.
10. What are the best curricula of these schools now

in use? In what respects are these (*a*) satisfactory, (*b*) unsatisfactory?

11. What should be the relation between the Sunday schools and the week-day church schools with respect to (*a*) pupils, (*b*) teachers, (*c*) curricula, (*d*) activities?

12. Give your own estimate of the future of week-day church schools.

Bibliography:

Cope—*The Week-Day Church School.* University of Chicago Press, Chicago, 1920.

Squires—*The Week-Day Church School.* Presbyterian Board of Publication, Philadelphia, 1920.

Wood—*School and College Credit for Outside Bible Study.* World Book Company, Yonkers, N. Y., 1917.

Wenner—*Religious Education and the Public School.* Bonnell, Silver & Co., New York, 1907.

Stafford—*The Vacation Religious School.* The Abingdon Press, New York, 1921.

Seaman-Abernethy—*Week-Day Religious Instruction as Conducted at Gary, Indiana.* Copyright 1921.

Richardson—*Standards of Week-Day Religious Instruction.* Northwestern University Occasional Papers.

Stout—*Week-Day Religious Instruction.* Northwestern University Occasional Papers.

Cowles-Antrim—*Van Wert Plan of Week-Day Religious Instruction.* The Pioneer Press, Van Wert, Ohio, 1921.

Religious Education, especially February, 1916; December, 1920; December, 1921; February, 1922; April, 1922; June, 1922.

Pamphlets published by denominational boards promoting religious education.

Pamphlets published by The International Daily Vacation Bible School Association, Bible House, New York.

CHAPTER IX

RELIGIOUS EDUCATION IN HIGHER INSTITUTIONS OF LEARNING

DOES the human race really make progress or does it move around in a circle? Is it always beginning to achieve and never reaching the goal which seems at times to be so nearly attainable? An incident in the life of John H. Vincent[1] (1866) will illustrate the problem raised.

Evanston Sunday-School Institute.—Dr. Vincent says:

Yielding to the unanimous request of the students of Garrett Biblical Institute, I visited Evanston and held four sessions of a Sunday-School Institute there on Friday and Saturday, September 14th and 15th. All the preliminary arrangements had been made by a committee representing the Bible Institute, Northwestern University, Northwestern Female College, and the Methodist Episcopal Sunday-School of Evanston. . . .

On Sunday afternoon I was present at the opening of the Sunday-School Normal Department of the Northwestern Female College. Had the honor of delivering the introductory lecture of their course. More than sixty young ladies were present. The lecture was on "The Divine Origin of Scripture." An outline of it was placed on the blackboard. Professor Bugbee, the president of the college, is a practical Sunday-school man, and will carry on the normal course with great success. He has given it a place in the curriculum of the institution. We

---

[1] *The Sunday-School Journal*, November, 1866.

expect to see this feature introduced into all of our seminaries for young ladies.

The Institute at Evanston was the first of its kind ever held. The suspension of exercises in the university, college, and institute, the presence of students and their professors, the inauguration of a regular Sunday-School Teachers' Normal Course in the Female College—all these features mark a new era in the great Sunday-school work. The standard is being elevated. The energy and talent of the church are concentrating upon a mighty appliance. The coming men and women are preparing to give it an intelligent and hearty support. Let us take courage and go forward. The whole church must be identified with the Sunday school; and as the educational department of the church let it command our best talent and our united efforts.

What would have been his feelings at the time if he could have known that forty-six years would elapse before Garrett Biblical Institute should install a chair of religious education, and that seven more years would follow before Northwestern University, of which the Northwestern Female College became a part, should create a department of religious education? The "new day" when colleges and seminaries should prepare teachers of religion for the local church and community did not dawn when it was expected.

Early colleges in America.—Religious education was the predominant motive for founding the first college in the American colonies. Harvard was founded in 1636 for the purpose of preparing candidates for the ministry. William and Mary (1693), Yale (1701), Kings College (Columbia) 1754, and all of the other colonial colleges were founded primarily for religious purposes.

The following is a part of an advertisement published in the New York papers announcing the opening of King's College: "IV The chief thing that is arrived at in this College is, to teach and engage the children to *know God in Jesus Christ,* and to love and serve him in all *sobriety,* *Godliness,* and *Richness* of *Life* with a pure Heart and a Willing Mind, and to train them up in all Virtuous Habits, and all such useful Knowledge as may render them creditable to their Families and Friends, Ornaments to their Country, and useful to the Public Weal in their generation."[2]

Soon the purpose of these colleges was broadened to include preparation for other "learned professions" and preparation for living the life of "a gentleman" according to the standards of that day. The curriculum laid especial stress upon Hebrew, Greek, and Latin, but in addition offered mathematics, a little of "natural science," training in oratory, and general history. Ethics, philosophy, and Christian evidences predominated in the senior year while language work predominated in the other three. But early in the nineteenth century the main purpose of preparing ministerial candidates became a secondary purpose. However, the ideal of laying a foundation for life work in the learned professions and of imparting culture to prepare the favored few for an enjoyable thoughtful life of relative ease did not pass so soon. In fact, this ideal can command adherents in almost any faculty in a college of liberal arts to-day. It is not our purpose to discuss the merits of such an ideal, but simply to record the fact that it has persisted down to the present. Every attempt to lessen the requirements in the classics so as to permit

---

[1] Cubberley—*Public Education in the United States,* p. 201. Houghton Mifflin Company, publishers. Used by permission.

the student to take more of science and certain practical studies needed in everyday life has been opposed tenaciously by the supporters of this older ideal of culture. It is not uncommon to-day to find denominational colleges requiring for graduation twenty to thirty semester hours of foreign language study and advanced mathematics while making no requirement in psychology, Bible, religious education, and similar subjects.

Rise of the State universities.—But the rise of State universities had a profound effect upon modifying the curricula of the colleges. These were founded for the very practical purpose of preparing future citizens for their duties as participants in a democracy. They did not ignore the classical studies, but they at once became as much interested in agriculture and engineering as in Latin—in fact, more so; and the sciences were given a prominent place because of their practical value. The following table indicates the date of the beginning of the earliest universities under direct State control:[3]

1819 University of Virginia.
1820 University of Indiana.
1821 University of North Carolina (established in 1789).
1831 University of Alabama.
1835 University of Michigan.
1838 University of Vermont (originally chartered in 1791).

State institutions prepare teachers for public schools.—But the principal influence of the State universities and State normal schools upon the curriculum of the college with respect to religious education is due to their emphasis upon preparing public school-teachers for the State. What could be more necessary

---

[3] See Cubberley, *Public Education in the United States*, pp. 206, 207.

to the life of the State than the preparation of an adequate supply of competent public-school teachers? The State schools made large provision for this feature and the States also offered inducements, if not requirements, which persuaded the privately endowed institutions to do the same.

DENOMINATIONAL COLLEGES ALSO PREPARE TEACHERS FOR THE STATE BUT NOT FOR THE CHURCH

In 1915, when Walter S. Athearn made his investigation of present conditions of religious education in colleges, he received replies from 140 institutions, 76 of which were institutions endorsed by the American Association of Universities. Of these 140 institutions, 20 were under State control, 62 classified themselves as denominational, 14 indicated no affiliations, and the others designated in a variety of ways their relation to religion.

A survey of present conditions.—In the course of his report he says:

Practically all the colleges offer a group of subjects that would naturally be included in a well-balanced course of religious education, such as ethics, sociology, philosophy, and general psychology. Comparative religion, Christian missions, and church history are listed in most catalogues. The frequency of such courses as the psychology of religion, social pathology, rural sociology, and Christianity and modern social problems indicates a response to the demands of the times.

Perhaps the most surprising thing in the reports is the unanimity with which the independent and church colleges have responded to the state's demand for trained teachers for the public schools. Nearly all of the States grant certain concessions and privileges to colleges that conform to the standards established by the State Departments of Public Instruction. Departments of education and chairs of psychology and pedagogy have sprung up in nearly all the denominational colleges. In almost all catalogues examined there are listed such courses as history of education, educational psychology, child psychology, philosophy of education, principles of education, school administration and management, methodology, etc.

Ninety-eight colleges report related courses with an average of eight courses in each college, which could be used to advantage in building a program for religious education. The church colleges may well be proud of their splendid contribution to the training of the secular teachers of the nation; but they have not been equally responsive to the pleading of the churches for teachers of religion.[4]

Reasons for failure to meet the churches' needs. —The reasons for such a situation are many but chiefly the following: (1) A failure to appreciate the importance of trying to give every boy and girl in the land adequate instruction in religion; (2) a fear of having the college called a "Sunday school" if linked up in any way with the task of training Sunday-school teachers; (3) the inevitable opposition to displacing any features of work given in subjects of longer standing; (4) opposition to any courses such as economics and education which might be called "utilitarian" because calculated to help one earn his living as well as to enrich his mind; (5) lack of sufficient income to enter new fields; (6) the comparatively undeveloped state of the new science of methodology in the field of religious education.

Religious achievements of church colleges.— When a historian is estimating the factors which have

[4] *Religious Education*, October, 1915, p. 413. Used by permission,

exerted the most influence upon the nation in advancing the cause of Christian education, he will give the church colleges and seminaries a very high place. Since the earliest times they have trained the great majority of the ministers who have had a college education. They have down to the present been the most fertile field for the recruiting of ministers. They have contributed an overwhelming majority of Christian missionaries and a large proportion of the welfare workers in agencies allied to the church. They have enriched the home life of the nation, and have given some preparation to hundreds of thousands of Sunday-school teachers and workers in other fields.

All of this and more the historian can say concerning the contribution of privately endowed institutions to the cause of Christian education. But the colleges have made this contribution largely by indirect methods such as through atmosphere, the example of instructors, Christian viewpoint in interpretation of courses, and campus activities. They have taught "related courses" but they have not yet in any large way, except rarely, set before themselves the definite task of providing a community with the kind of skillful Christian workers which society in this day needs so greatly. These institutions are just beginning to accept this responsibility, and the acceptance of it in theory is by no means unanimous yet. Within the last two years a college president stated as follows: "I have taught religion to college students for twenty-five years, and as far as affecting character is concerned, it has been a great disappointment. Pastoral work, the personal touch is the great thing at our State universities and private colleges as well." Another college president, progressive on most points, about the same time declared "the present emphasis upon religious education is a fad and will soon pass."

DEVELOPMENT OF BIBLE STUDY AND RELIGIOUS EDUCATION

The field in which the denominational colleges have made their most direct contribution to religious education within the past twenty years has been in Bible study. Since 1900 the number of institutions which have installed chairs of Bible study has increased rapidly until to-day it is rare to find a church college which does not offer accredited courses in Bible, and practically all of them will accept a limited amount of entrance credits in Bible. The catalogues of forty-two white colleges of the Methodist Episcopal Church of the year 1919–1920, including the theological seminaries of Boston University and Garrett Biblical Institute, affiliated with Northwestern University, showed 748 semester hours of Bible offered. Clearly the Bible has won a conspicuous place in the curricula of these institutions. These catalogues also showed 810 semester hours in Education: 554 in Psychology, 143 in Philosophy of Religion. However, only 15 of the colleges offered any courses in Religious Education with a total of 154 semester hours. Omitting Boston and Northwestern together with Garrett Biblical Institute only 51 semester hours were offered according to these catalogues checked up by letters and telegrams. Confusion of nomenclature was noted and five more colleges offered courses in Evangelism, Sunday-School Theory and Practice, which would bring the total to 234 semester hours. Again, deducting for Northwestern and Boston we get only 114 hours. It should be said, however, that several of these institutions began work in religious education in

1920–21. In December, 1921, 37 white colleges of this denomination taken from the same group, but omitting Garrett Biblical Institute, the Boston School of Theology, and the School of Religion and Social Service of Boston University, reported 658 semester hours in Bible with 3,669 students, while 29 instead of 20 (as in 1920) report 375 semester hours in religious education with 1,052 students. Deducting duplicates, 4,270 students were taking either Bible or Religious Education in these institutions, while in the same institutions 5,859 were taking advantage of 1,149 semester hours offered in general education. This clearly shows a great gain of interest within the past two years. Two more great institutions of this denomination established chairs of Religious Education in the fall of 1922.

To meet the need for textbooks to be used in college courses a very significant series was prepared especially for this purpose under the joint editorship of Dr. John T. McFarland and Dr. David G. Downey. The first books in this series that appeared were: *The Bible as Literature*, Wood-Grant, and *New Testament History*, Rall; both published in September, 1914. *Old Testament History*, Peritz, and *Social Institutions and Ideals of the Bible*, Soares, followed. The quality of these books helped in many places to overcome the criticism that religion could not be taught in colleges on a par with other subjects.

Influence of psychologists.—The cause of religious education owes much to the development of the new science of psychology and the directing of psychological investigation into the field of religion. *The Psychology of Religion*, Starbuck (1899), and *The Spiritual Life*, Coe (1900), created a sensation in religious circles. The application of psychological laboratory methods in the field of religious experience seemed to some to be as sacrilegious as touching the ark was to the ancient Hebrews. But it created a new interest in religion in university circles, and the most forward-looking church workers also welcomed these methods of scientific research. Just as the application of scientific methods to the study of biblical literature aroused a great interest in Bible study in the universities in the last quarter of the past century—an interest that is still strong—so the new science of the psychology of religion in the first quarter of the new century has proved to be a great asset to religion. That Christianity has suffered more from indifference than it ever has from opposition and false theories is too apparent to require comment. Without passing any judgment upon many theories advanced both in the field of biblical research and that of the psychology of religion, we are simply stating that both of these movements gave an unmistakable impetus to the study of religion, and have been invaluable assets to the promotion of religious education.

Many brilliant psychologists made a great contribution to religious education in the years 1900 to 1910. In addition to the two writers previously mentioned, such men as William James, G. Stanley Hall, and others were especially stimulating and suggestive. The creators and writers of the International Graded Lessons in some of the series relied much upon the investigations of these men.

Influence of the Religious Education Association. —One must also give considerable credit to the influence of the Religious Education Association, which from the beginning has exerted more influence upon the college instructors and administrators than upon any other constituency. The college men who were the leading spirits of this organization found in the conventions and in the magazine of this Association very useful channels for propaganda in behalf of Bible study and other phases of Christian instruction.

Theological seminaries and colleges.—The leading theological seminaries became heartily committed to the teaching of the principles, materials, and methods of religious education in the first fifteen years of the twentieth century.

There was practically no opposition to a chair of religious education in theological seminaries after the awakening at the beginning of the century. The installing of such chairs became largely a matter of when the institution could secure first the necessary funds and then the properly trained men. But the installation of such chairs in the colleges was a much slower development, carried on in the face of stubborn opposition. At the present writing it seems as if the opposition has just about yielded to the new movement. College administrators may not favor any vocational courses in the college, but they are generally willing to concede that religious education has as good a right to a place in the curriculum as secular education, now so generally introduced.

Religious education at State universities.—It may seem anomalous to suggest that one of the most potent factors for the promotion of departments of religious education in privately endowed institutions within the last five years has been the example of State universities and their affiliated organizations. Years ago when the battle for church or State control of the public schools was on, the State-controlled public schools were referred to as "godless." Later this phrase as applied to the public schools was dropped by Protestants and this opprobrium was given to the State universities. Loyal church members were exhorted not to send their children to these "godless" institutions. But the advantages of free tuition, well-equipped laboratories, and vocational training courses, advantages lacking in part at least in many church schools, were too strong an inducement, and thousands of parents failed to heed the warning.

The State universities enjoyed a phenomenal growth, while all but the strongest of privately endowed institutions found themselves struggling to maintain their work at its former standard of relative excellence and popularity. The majority of privately endowed institutions had little money to invest in such new courses as those in religious education even if they had had the disposition to do so. Furthermore, the Christian traditions of their colleges, and the Christian character of almost every member of the faculty, led the leaders of these institutions to feel that the one item which was most certainly provided for was religious instruction, even if it was left out of the curriculum as a definite course.

On the other hand, the Christian leaders who were interested in the success of the State universities recognized that some definite guidance and instruction in religion was necessary if the students of these institutions were to play their part in the Christianization of the world. Various methods were devised to meet this need. The first one emphasized by church leaders was the development of the local churches so that they could serve the religious interests of the students. Such a program seemed to require satisfactory preaching, a strong young people's devotional meeting, and occasional socials. This program is still satisfactory to many Christian ministers and to some educational leaders, although candor compels the statement that most of these are not located at the seats of State universities.

Another plan, coming from the university authorities, called for teaching Biblical literature and history in such departments as English, Semitics, or Greek, and the introduction of some religious materials in such departments as Ethics, Sociology, and Philosophy. Undoubtedly much wholesome religious instruction has been given in this way, but the instructors must necessarily work under limitations which preclude their giving an adequate amount of definite religious training. The University of Texas, the University of Michigan, and the University of Washington are typical of universities which have adopted this method.

A third plan provides for a union college of religion located on the campus of the university or adjacent to it, and closely affiliated with the university. In this plan several denominations unite to support the college while the university lends assistance in every possible way and awards credits under specified conditions for courses taken in the College of Religion. This plan has been in successful operation in the State University of Missouri and is being undertaken at the University of Wisconsin. A fourth plan has been to develop a denominational college adjacent to the campus of the State University and in affiliation with the university. Wesley College, a pioneer institution of this type, was established adjacent to the University of North Dakota in 1899. It has had a very honorable career, and its success has been an important factor in influencing the denominations to establish institutions which will teach religion in affiliation with State universities.

Wesley Foundation, University of Illinois.—A plan which has had conspicuous success at the University of Illinois thus far and seems to be only at the beginning of its achievement, is really a combination of the first and last plans described. Sixteen years ago James C. Baker went to Urbana, Illinois, to build up a church for the university constituency only. Many questioned the wisdom of the plan. The existing churches did not wish to give up any of their adherents, and the problem of finance loomed large. By patient, resourceful, devoted work this institution was built up until the church building erected in 1906 became utterly inadequate. A group of new buildings to include a church, a social center, with library, as well as dormitories for men and women were projected and on February 15, 1921, the first of the new buildings, a social center, was dedicated. A staff of three men give full time to the work, and one of these teaches courses in Bible and religious education, which are accredited by the university.

At the dedication exercises President Kinley, of the university, said, "To my mind no education is complete which does not include religious education."

In presenting the building to be dedicated Dr. Baker said, "We dedicate this building to the service of God and the cause of religious education." The number of students actually enrolled in credit courses offered by the Wesley Foundation at the University of Illinois in the school year 1921–1922, was 168. The additional number of students enrolled in Sunday-school (voluntary) classes was 467. Dr. Baker writes under date of January 3, 1922: "Please remember that we are only at the beginning of our credit work. . . . We are much encouraged and expect the classes to grow in numbers as the idea gets into the student consciousness."

Such a movement on the campuses of State universities could not fail to act as a powerful stimulant upon privately endowed institutions. In the writer's hearing, one college president in opposing support for such enterprises at State universities said, "Give our school the money which people are trying to raise for this religious foundation at ———, and I can keep the [naming his denomination] students away from that university." Another, deliberately addressing a conference of educational leaders, backed up his opposition against giving denominational aid to such an enterprise by saying, "If these plans as constituted go through, the students at this State university will have better religious advantages than they have at ———," naming a strong church school.

But one can hardly object to a denomination making adequate provision for teaching religion on the campus of a university where as at the University of Illinois 1920–1921, two thousand four hundred and ninety-seven adherents of this denomination were in attendance and the number growing each year.

The purpose of the religious foundations at State universities is essentially religious education. The other features of instruction are already provided for by the universities. The real difference of opinion seems to be as to whether or not religious education is a necessity to university students, some believing that satisfactory preaching and ample opportunities for devotional and social expression will be sufficient.

Despite opposition these religious foundations are making headway and are gradually winning the approval of denominational college presidents and other educational leaders.

The college Y. M. C. A. and Y. W. C. A.—Another religious factor of very large importance in the colleges and universities is found in the Young Men's Christian Association and the Young Women's Christian Association. These hold great summer conferences annually which enlist many of the ablest students to volunteer for life-service as professional Christian workers, and which practically infuse enough inspiration and suggestions to keep Christian activities going at high pressure throughout the next school year. On the whole, for the last twenty-five years they have given more members of the student body training for some phase of Christian work than all of the other agencies in a college community combined.

With the new interest in training for Christian service coming to the front, it is not to be expected that the Christian Associations will maintain or desire to maintain any such monopoly, but they must be credited with providing much instruction and training which the college faculties and the churches should have provided. They will undoubtedly continue their great service of inspiration and guidance, but will share the responsibility in the future. Their system of volunteer Bible-study classes has done much to raise the ideals of students, but as a system of study it has been no match for the accredited courses. The result has been that the student has studied carefully his Latin, mathematics, chemistry, and English literature, but has studied the Bible or missionary problems in only the most superficial way, if, indeed, he has studied these problems at all.

GRADUATE DEPARTMENTS OF RELIGIOUS EDUCATION IN UNIVERSITIES

While the colleges have been very reluctant to match their courses in general education with courses in religious education, a few of the great privately endowed universities have within the last few years equipped themselves so that they offer graduate degrees in religious education. Professor Athearn[5] in the report previously cited mentions Columbia University, the University of Chicago, and Yale College as the only institutions offering the degree of Doctor of Philosophy with a major in religious education in 1915.

The University of Chicago deserves credit as a pioneer in this field. The University of Chicago Press issued one of the first series of completely graded Sunday-school lessons, and, in fact, William Rainey Harper, former president of the institution, backed the Blakeslee Graded Lessons before he became president of the university. As far back as 1899 he conceived the plan of providing a series of textbooks for the study of the Bible, which should be adapted for all ages, to meet the needs of several periods of life from the kindergarten to adulthood. The first volume was brought out in 1900, and in 1906, upon his death, Professor E. D. Burton became the editor. Eventually, after the International Graded Lessons had been launched, this series was completed as the Constructive Bible Series.

Teachers College, Columbia, has offered advanced degrees with a major in religious education since 1911. The affiliation of Union Theological Seminary with this institution, affords the student excellent opportunities for graduate study in this field. In 1922 Professor

---

[5] *Religious Education*, October, 1915, p. 46.

George Albert Coe resigned from the Seminary in order to give all of his time to Teachers' College. He was succeeded by Harrison S. Elliott. Attention should also be called to the Hartford School of Religious Pedagogy, which, under the leadership of Edward Porter St. John, blazed a trail in this field.

The Theological School, Boston University, established a chair of religious education in 1911. In 1916 the faculty was substantially enlarged under the leadership of Norman E. Richardson until the department was offering 48 semester hours of work in religious education. In 1919 this enlarged department was organized as a School of Religious Education under Walter S. Athearn, director. This school and the affiliated School of Theology offered 325 semester hours in Bible, 155 in religious education, enrolling 278 students for the school year 1921–1922. One hundred of these were full-time students taking work in this school of Boston University only. Fifty-two out of the total number enrolled were graduate students. It also conducts extensive laboratory experiments in the vicinity of Boston such as the Malden Community School, organized in 1917.

In 1919 Norman E. Richardson resigned as head of the Department of Religious Education of Boston School of Theology, going to Northwestern University. With him in the department were associated George Herbert Betts and later John E. Stout, both famous in the field of public-school education. Northwestern at the same time, 1919, secured Edmund D. Soper as professor of history of missions, and Albert E. Bailey for a chair in rural sociology. These accessions to the faculty of Northwestern plus the professors in Garrett Biblical Institute and the college instructors in education gave Northwestern unusual resources for taking a place of leadership in the new movement. Among the most significant contributions of the department thus far are the promotion of experimental week-day schools of religion in Evanston, Illinois, Hammond, Indiana, and Oak Park, Illinois, of Community Training Schools, and the preparation of curriculum material for both of these types of schools. In 1921 over 5,000 children were receiving week-day religious instruction in the experimental centers directed by this department.

COMMISSION ON RELIGIOUS EDUCATION IN COLLEGES

On January 29, 1920, at its annual meeting in Saint Louis, Missouri, the Sunday-School Council of Evangelical Denominations requested the Council of Church Boards of Education to appoint a committee which would act with the Sunday-School Council's representatives as a Joint Committee on Teacher Training in Colleges for the purpose of standardizing and stimulating the work in this field. This action was taken at the request of the Teacher-Training Committee of the Council, the members of which felt that the next great forward movement in religious education must inevitably be held back until the colleges begin sending into the local communities a stream of people who are equipped for teaching and other forms of Christian service.

After working for a year and preparing a Report of Progress to submit to their respective bodies, it was discovered that the Religious Education Association had appointed a commission under the chairmanship of George Albert Coe, to deal with substantially the same problems. The two committees at once exchanged information and assembled in joint session at the Convention of the Religious Education Association in Rochester, New York, March 11, 1921. The first joint session was an open one, to which all the instructors of Bible or of religious education, together with other guests, were invited. The remaining sessions were private. It was found that these two committees working separately were proceeding along practically the same lines and were in almost complete agreement upon the major points. The following is the report of the Joint Commission as it was adopted by the Council of Church Boards of Education and the Sunday-School Council of Evangelical Denominations.[6]

Recommendations of Joint Commission:—

I. That colleges upon religious foundations pursue the policy of offering sufficient work in Bible, the Christian religion, and various subjects related to religious education to prepare their students for intelligent support and leadership of religious education in their home churches and communities.

II. That the total amount of work contemplated as a minimum be one fourth of a four years' college course, or in the usual terminology of the colleges, thirty semester hours.

III. That the subjects and the approximate number of hours allotted to each subject be:

1. Bible........................... 6 semester hours
2. Teaching Values of Bible material... 3 " "
3. Curriculum...................... 2 " "
4. The Christian Religion............ 3 " "
5. Educational Psychology.......... 3 " "
6. Introduction to the Study of Religious Education................ 3 " "

[6] These organizations modified the original report adopted by the Religious Education Association by making the basis of certificate recognition 24 semester hours, instead of 30, and by indicating that 19 of these hours should be in required subjects.

7. Teaching the Christian religion (with
   observation and practice)........ 4 semester hours
8. Organization and Administration... 3   "   "
9. History of Religious Education in
   America...................... 3   "   "
   ___
   Total.................30 semester hours

IV. That a certificate in religious education be granted to students who, upon graduation, have completed a total of 24 semester hours of work herein described, 19 of which shall be in required courses and 5 of which may be elected from the remaining courses indicated in "III." The required courses will be:

Bible............................. 6 semester hours
The Christian Religion.............. 3   "   "
Educational Psychology............. 3   "   "
Introduction to the Study of Religious
   Education...................... 3   "   "
Teaching the Christian Religion (with
   observation and practice)......... 4   "   "

Content and Emphasis.

While not desiring to outline any courses, the Joint Commission further offers the following suggestions with reference to content and emphasis in each subject.

1. *Bible.*

The aim should be an intelligent appreciation of the Bible as a whole, understanding of the historical situations represented in its various parts, realization of the permanent significance of its great messages, and readiness to use its resources for the needs of to-day. In presenting this subject, the method of bare outlines should be avoided; rather, the general perspective should be made vivid by detailed study of a few typical parts, and students should be trained in the use of the sources.

2. *Teaching Values of Bible Material.*

The necessity for instruction upon this topic grows out

of two considerations: The great extent and variety of
the biblical literature and the wide difference between
pupils in point of experience and spiritual need. The
Word of Truth must be "rightly divided." Hence, (1)
Specific material must be selected to fit different ages
and needs. In this matter good judgment is required of
the teacher as well as of curriculum makers. (2) Within
the material thus selected, the specifically Christian
values must be apprehended and brought into the fore-
ground. These requirements necessitate a canvassing of
the more significant portions of the Scriptures with such
questions as these in mind: For what ages is this passage
appropriate? What problems of Christian living might
it help solve? Viewed from the standpoint of the mind
of Christ, what is the main point?

3. *Curriculum.*

This should be a study both of existing curricula and
of the principles of curriculum making. Especial attention should be given to a study of how to select the right
curricula not only for particular schools, but also for
particular classes within the schools.

4. *The Christian Religion.*

An objective study of the Christian religion in the
twentieth century, including the essentials of Christian
living, what the churches are actually doing in their
effort to Christianize every phase of life, and their program for the future, beginning in the local community,
and reaching out to the remotest and most inaccessible
parts of the world.

5. *Educational Psychology.*

The usual courses in educational psychology can be
made suitable for teachers of religion by a few modifications. Indeed, the problems of public-school teachers and
of church-school teachers are almost identical in such
matters as original nature, interest, and attention, habit
formation, memory, thinking, transfer of training, fatigue,
and individual differences. But the subject of motivation

needs more attention than it commonly receives—motivation not merely in the pupil's approach to particular school subjects, but also and especially in the formation of life purposes as a citizen and as a member of a religious communion. In the study of original nature, native tendencies that underlie social and anti-social attitudes and conduct are of predominant importance. The analysis of habit should not omit the formation and the transformation of likes and dislikes, opinions, prejudices, loyalties, and ideals. How a self is formed, and how group minds are formed and modified are likewise essential problems.

6. *Introduction to the Study of Religious Education.*

The purpose of this study should be not only to develop a broad outlook upon the meaning of education in general and of religious education in particular, but also to give point to thought and planning with respect to practical issues of our day. The specific aims of Christian education should be made clear, and likewise the place of education in the Christian plan for the reconstruction of society. The aims and methods of Christian education should be compared with those of the public schools, and the respective educational functions of the church, the family, and the state should be considered. The philosophy that underlies particular types of religious education should be made clear. Finally, the child's relation to God, the nature and process of religious growth, the meaning of worship (with the educational use of it), and the meaning of church membership, should be included.

7. *Teaching the Christian Religion* (Observation Work and Practice Teaching included).

The student of method needs to learn what methods of teaching religion now in use succeed, and why they succeed. This implies not only familiarity with general standards for judging teaching, but also acquaintance with the details of the various processes involved. Training in making lesson plans, in story-telling, in questioning, and in observing children should be required. Wherever observation of teaching and practice in teaching can be properly supervised, they should be included.

8. *Organization and Administration.*

One of the most difficult, and likewise fruitful, fields of Christian service in our generation is the organization and direction of the available educational energies of the churches. The former restricted conception of building a Sunday school is now broadened to include instruction on Sunday, on week days, also in vacation time, and likewise a multitude of activities and groupings of children and young people. Moreover, the point from which to view all this is no longer the isolated church society, but groups of churches, the community, whole denominations, nation-wide and world-wide agencies. College students need to know what is happening in these directions, and they need to know it in such concreteness and detail that they will be able to take the lead in the educational organization of their own churches and communities.

9. *History of Religious Education in America.*

The special problems of teaching and of organization have their setting in a larger whole, namely, the life of the churches, the life of the nation, and changing social conditions. The worker must see his work in this perspective, or he will not grasp its full significance. He needs particularly to understand contemporary developments of religious education in his own country; the history of the Sunday school in America, especially the reform movement of the twentieth century and its forerunners; the setting of the Sunday school in the larger whole of religious and moral education; the secularization of the public schools—why it occurred, and what the present laws and policies are with respect thereto; developments in the educational outlook and work of the churches and of communities as determined by growing knowledge and by social changes—these topics are of immeasurable importance to the Christian citizen of either the United States or Canada.

Relation to Other Subjects of Study.

The Commission would emphasize the point that what is here proposed is not a course of training for professional workers in religious education; much less is it a theological course or a substitute for one. It is hoped and believed that out of the studies here sketched will arise frequently an interest and ambition to give one's whole life to one or another Christian calling as an occupation. The Commission has not felt called upon to raise the question of what further opportunities the colleges might possibly offer to such students. Our recommendations are limited to the minimum that seems to us necessary in order that our people may understand the Christian culture that they inherit and the rudiments of Christian living in the world of to-day.

Who Should Teach These Subjects?

The treatment of religious education should not be less serious, thorough, and technical than the treatment that "general" education receives. In both fields technically equipped specialists are required as teachers. A temptation will arise to intrust some or all of the subjects that have been named to the "handy man" of the faculty; or to append them as secondary duties to the schedules of teachers whose training and first interests lie elsewhere; or to appoint someone as teacher on the ground of availability and cheapness; or to group existing courses that deal with the Bible, religion, and education, and call them "religious education." Administrators should clearly understand that what is required is not a new name for an old thing, nor merely new permutations and combinations of courses and students. Our recommendation concerns a new branch of study with specific aims and subject matter of its own, together with a new approach to certain older subjects. Effective education in this field cannot begin too soon, for the need is tragically imperative; yet it would be less evil to wait indefinitely for proper conditions of income, teaching staff, and library, than to substitute anything whatever for high grade teaching.

Respectfully submitted by the Committee.

It is significant that the Minutes of the First Annual Meeting of the Sunday-School Council of Evangelical Denominations 1911, record the following resolution:

I. On The Training of Sunday-School Workers in Our Colleges and Seminaries.

Recognizing with gladness the work already done in some of our Colleges and Seminaries.

Resolved: (1) That we urge the establishment of lectures and study courses, dealing with the English Bible, religious pedagogy, and allied topics, and that such courses be made a part of the regular curriculum in all our secondary schools, colleges, and theological seminaries.

(2) That wherever possible we urge the establishment in all these institutions of full professorships, dealing with these subjects, and professorships in each institution to be of equal standing with any other professorship in the same institution.

(3) That we recommend to our theological seminaries the establishment of special courses for the training of superintendents, teachers, and other Sunday-school workers.

(4) That the various Sunday-School Boards or Societies represented in this Council will cooperate in every possible way with the aforesaid schools, colleges, and seminaries in the establishment of said courses and professorships.

II. On The Training of Sunday-school Workers in State and Other Higher Institutions of Learning.

(1) That the Council has learned with gratitude of the introduction of departments of Religious Pedagogy

and of lectureships on modern Sunday-school principles and practice into State and other institutions of learning, and expresses the hope that such instruction may be made permanent in the institutions where it exists and extended throughout the continent.

(2) That the Sunday-School Boards here represented pledge their active cooperation with the student pastors resident near said institutions in all wise efforts to train the students under their charge for skilled leadership in the home Sunday school.

Perhaps the interest has not developed as rapidly as some might have wished. But on the whole very substantial development has taken place, and the institutions of higher learning are to-day beginning to adopt whole-heartedly some program for the training of teachers and other workers in religious education.[7]

SUMMARY

We have traced briefly the progress of religious education as a subject for curricular study in the institutions of higher learning of the United States from colonial days down to the present. In the earliest period we noted that training in religion was a predominant interest and that later it was almost dropped as an aim of the denominational colleges of liberal arts. We noted that even the theological seminaries of the last century did not undertake to prepare students directly for the religious educational work of the church.

---

[7] Since 1916, under the leadership of John W. Shackford, the Board of Sunday-Schools and the Board of Education of the Methodist Episcopal Church, South, have been granting certificates to college students in schools of their denomination on a basis similar to that recommended by this joint commission. In fact, the successful work of these agencies was a very significant influence in furthering the work of the commission. The cooperation of the colleges of the Southern Baptist Convention, with Sunday-school agencies, in teacher training has also been significant.

However, the new day so long delayed, dawned early in the twentieth century and we have found that especially in the last ten years steps have been taken not only in privately endowed institutions, but also in State universities to teach religion as a curricular subject so as to prepare students for church and community service as religious workers. Years will be required before the body of literature available for students in this field is adequate. But no one can deny that those who apply themselves to this field of scientific investigation are studying one of the most vital aspects of life either from the standpoint of culture or from that of social efficiency. The development has been so marked during the last decade that a few cannot escape the feeling that it may be a fad. However, the evidence based upon the needs of students and the substantial support being given on every hand indicate that this development is only in its beginning. Whenever our higher institutions of learning actually contribute to the world a great company of young people who are competent to teach religion either as parents, volunteer workers, or as professional instructors, then a new day of moral advance will dawn for the world.

Questions for discussion:

1. How do you account for the fact that the colleges organized in the early days of American history had so much interest in training for religious work while the colleges at the beginning of the twentieth century seemed to have comparatively so little?

2. Why was the development which seemed to Dr. Vincent to be so imminent in 1866 postponed fifty years?

3. How did the rise of State universities affect the teaching of religion in colleges of liberal arts?

4. How do you account for the reluctance of the denominational colleges of liberal arts for many years to teach religion as a curricular subject?

5. Cite examples of colleges which are teaching religion for credit, giving a history of these developments and their results.

6. What have been the principal contributions to the cause of religion on the part of the denominational colleges within the last fifty years?

7. What is your estimate of the success of the courses in Bible as taught to-day in typical colleges?

8. How do you account for the present rapidly growing interest in religious education as a curricular subject for colleges and graduate schools?

9. What plans for teaching religion at State universities or in affiliation with them do you believe will be most successful in the next ten years?

10. Do you expect to see a rapid development of departments of religion in graduate schools during the next fifteen years? Why?

11. What is the outlook for religious education in the colleges of the United States as you see it?

Brief bibliography for special reference:

Religious Education, current and old files, especially report on "Religious Education as a Profession," October, 1915, and "Report of Commission on Religious Education in Colleges," December, 1921.

Reports of Denominational Boards of Education.

Reports of Council of Church Boards of Education.

Reports of Committee on Education, International Sunday-School Council of Religious Education, held in Kansas City, June, 1922.

Discussions in the periodical press.

CHAPTER X

PRESENT TENDENCIES IN RELIGIOUS EDUCATION

A FORETELLER not only is without honor in his own country but will probably never come to any great honor abroad. This chapter makes no attempt at prediction, but it does undertake to describe present tendencies. Many people would like to know about the future of religious education in America. Letters have very frequently come to the writer asking what are the prospects that lie before one if he takes up religious education as a lifework. Who knows? The present tendencies indicate a career of great usefulness to those whose natural gifts and adequate training have fitted them for success in this field.

A new appreciation of need.—But we will not predict. The outlook was almost as bright in 1867 as it is to-day. A terrific upheaval had shaken American life to its depths. Men everywhere realized that unless a race could be developed which would know and practice the ideals of Jesus, there was little hope of ever seeing a happy world. Much was accomplished toward the realization of this hope, and the nation emerged from that period far better equipped than ever before to provide religious training for all. But the development of an adequate system of religious instruction for the nation did not come as the leaders of that day fondly hoped. Such may also be the outcome of the efforts of the present generation of leaders.

But at present the conditions are more favorable

than in any former period. There is apparently an appreciation of the importance of religious instruction for the young which has never existed before. The horrors of the recent World War have made clear the tragedy of expecting a happy world through the achievements of a perfected human mechanism known as the "superman." The suffering caused by the so-called "Peace" of Versailles has made clear that the religious idealist is perhaps not so impractical as the one who claims to deal only with hard facts, and tries to exact the pound of flesh from a prostrate foe. The horrors of starvation, plunder, and murder brought about through the terrorism of a despotic minority in Russia have revealed the fact that self-interest, even though it speaks in terms of brotherhood for a limited class, is no adequate motive for rebuilding a prostrate country.

ADEQUATE MOTIVATION REQUIRES RELIGION

No one has expressed the need better than Rabindranath Tagore, although he may be unfair to the agency when he says of the League of Nations: "It is founded on force—it has no spiritual foundation. Humanity is not yet ready for it. A new machine is of little advantage if it is run by the old power for the old ends. Organization is not brotherhood, and God cares more for a brother than he does for an empire. The Great War was one of the blows of God seeking to break down our materialism, our selfishness, our narrow nationalisms. It made a dent, but only a dent in the crust. Other blows will fall betimes until we learn to live together by the real law of our nature— Law of Love—a veil will hide the beauty and wonder of the world, leaving us to wander alone or struggle together in confusion and strife." Many readers will join the writer in hoping that either the present or another League of Nations will make sure that it has a spiritual foundation, for permanent peace can come in no other way.

The political chaos, the industrial unrest, the business instability, all point unquestionably to the need of a spiritual quality in human life, a quality which Christian nurture, where faithfully tried, has been able to develop. Public-school educators are emphasizing motivation as a *sine qua non* for successful learning. The development of right attitudes is one of the main tasks of a teacher. Educational processes must be tested by conduct. Little wonder, then, that the attention of leaders is turning to the problem of motivation. But where do we find an adequate motive for brotherly conduct? Certainly not in self-interest, however much "enlightened" it may be. As a matter of fact, in history most of the people who have had such a motive have found it in love for a Person whom they believed to be the Son of God who is the Father of the human race. This fact is profoundly influencing the policies of leading educators to-day, and seems destined to wield still greater influence in the near future. Even though they may be uncertain about the absolute reality of the Father God, they cannot deny that the world needs one, and that faith in him has been the most powerful incentive to brotherly conduct that the world has ever known.

Direct teaching of religion a necessity.—Should proof be required that the direct teaching of religion to the young is a necessity if the race is ever to become intelligent about religion, it could be found in the ignorance on religious subjects of the American and British soldiers in the World War. These men, most of them, came from so-called "Christian countries." Many of them were raised in Christian homes and had been frequently in Sunday-school and other church services. But the actual facts about the development of the religion of Jesus, about the teachings of Jesus and the working program of the churches were all very hazy items to them. The published reports of careful investigations of the religion of army men have been strong factors in creating a nation-wide feeling of need. And the first-hand evidence given so universally by the chaplains and soldiers themselves has been still more effective. It is reasonable to claim that the thinking people of America see the need for an adequate system of religious education for the nation to-day as never before.

Separation and cooperation between church and state.—As to whether or not such a system can be produced in harmony with the principle of separation between church and state, there is considerable doubt, with the tendency strongly inclining toward .hope and confidence. This confidence arises from two causes. In the first place, because the cases of cooperation in particular cities have been sufficiently numerous and successful to warrant confidence. In the second place, because groups of workers interested in both education and religion have come to understand and cooperate with each other better. The more mystically inclined religious workers are losing their fear of religious education as a merely mechanical substitute for an emotional change of motive and a passionate loyalty to Jesus Christ, while the educational leaders are coming to appreciate the value of religion to education as they have not done before in recent years.

The newer educational leaders are just as much opposed to any formal, mechanical processes of character development as any mystic can be. Even if they have no place for God in their thinking, they define education as "the progressive reconstruction of experience," and a change of motive, familiarly known in religious circles as "a change of heart," is no unthinkable experience to them. They expect such and really seek to produce a change of motive frequently. The Christian, when building upon this theory of education, finds love for the Father as revealed in Jesus the most powerful incentive for the cultivation of reverence, honesty, desire to serve, loyalty, and other virtuous attitudes.

The outstanding difference between Christian educators and educational leaders who have no faith in God is just here. One group use the stories about God and his helpers to inspire an adequate motive for social usefulness. They also use every other available means to develop in the pupil a consciousness of fellowship with God and a passionate loyalty to Christian ideals in society. The other educators seek to develop right attitudes, even Christian ideals and skill in social service, without any reference to faith in God as revealed by Jesus Christ.

THE PRINCIPAL AGENCIES

What agencies will the Christian educator use in seeking to achieve his purpose? He will use every means available, but the instruments most practical for his purpose are the home, the school—Sunday and week-day school—the college, and the graduate school. The present tendency is to lay the greatest possible emphasis upon all four.

The Sunday school.—Thus far the Sunday school has gone the farthest toward perfecting its technique as an agency for the direct teaching of religion. Few will deny that down to the present the Sunday school is more nearly a school of religion than any other feature of the local church. Its leaders from one end of the country to the other have the school ideal, and they have brought the curriculum and methodology to a state where a reasonably faithful use of these will actually produce gratifying educational results.

Other organizations within the church, such as the Christian Endeavor, the Epworth League, and the special missionary societies, are zealously endeavoring to develop a satisfactory educational technique for their work. The effort is highly gratifying, for every church should have one unified educational program under the direction of a committee and the proper supervisors. The more nearly these organizations approach the same educational standards and methods as the modernized Sunday and week-day church school, the easier it will be to set up a real school system in an individual church.

Week-day church schools.—Meantime, while the Sunday-school leaders are perfecting the Sunday school, they are also experimenting and promoting week-day church schools. Ideally one might hope that all of the Protestant churches could unite to establish and operate plants for the teaching of religion under an able corps of instructors adjacent to every public school building. The pupils would then come to the church schools according to a carefully adjusted schedule for a study of the religious materials and beliefs which are common to all of Protestantism. On Sunday in their own Sunday schools they would learn the history and the peculiar tenets of their own denominations, with especial attention given to the program of world service in which they are expected to take part as church members.

Actually, however, religious education among Protestants will probably come in one of the following ways: In some communities the churches which are most congenial will unite to conduct common schools of religion, whether this union embraces all or only two individual congregations. Elsewhere individual congregations will conduct their own week-day schools independently, except that they may unite with other churches to arrange a satisfactory time schedule with the public-school authorities. It seems clear to the writer that religion is too important a subject to be taught after public-school hours, and that when public sentiment on this subject is crystallized in a given community there will be no doubt concerning the wisdom of giving this instruction at a time when the pupil is unfatigued. That the public-school authorities will gladly cooperate to this end when a community really becomes interested in religious education seems to be certain.

Future of the Sunday schools.—The Sunday school seems to be just at the beginning of its career of usefulness, rather than at the end of it, as some have supposed. Although the time granted to it is altogether too short, if it has an hour and a half before 10:45 Sunday morning, it has one of the most favorable periods of the week—a period when it faces no competition except that of indifference and inertia. People of all ages and of all occupations are to-day receiving valuable instruction at this period. The materials and the technique of this institution have improved so within the last fifteen years that where they are used by a competent teacher the Sunday school is one of the most powerful influences in the lives of those who are reached by it. It is doubtful if any single hour and a half during the week goes further toward shaping ideals and developing moral habits than this hour in a Sunday school under competent, even though volunteer, leadership.

Will the Sunday-school teachers of the future be paid? Yes and no. The supervisors of teachers will be paid so far as possible, and an increasing number of teachers. But the church can never afford to lose the volunteer services of hundreds of thousands of great Christian laymen who cannot make religious teaching a vocation, but who are glad to perfect themselves as teachers for part-time service. The impact upon social movements of this great company of worthy officers and teachers is one of the most powerful forces for righteousness in the world to-day. The company should be increased in number and improved in ability and spirit but never allowed to disband.

On the other hand, the week-day schools of religion will require the full time of many workers. And a great company of teachers and supervisors with the highest professional standards must be developed for this work.

The Christian college.—As we have noted, the Christian college has for some years been preparing teachers for the state to use in its public schools, and has just begun to show a similar interest in preparing them for the church to use in its schools of religion. No one seems to question what the future policy will be in this matter. Whether most of the colleges will give a vocational degree, Bachelor of Religious Education, or offer the necessary courses and accredit the work toward the Bachelor of Arts or Bachelor of Science degree, is uncertain, because both policies are being tried at present. But undoubtedly the colleges will offer the most essential courses in religion for credit.

The majority of Christians will probably agree that in developing a new generation for social efficiency, so that it will be competent to remake the world according to the ideals of Jesus, the direct teaching of religious facts and principles, is an indispensable element.

Graduate schools of religion.—But the college will not assume responsibility for completing the professional training of leaders in religion. The college will do its largest service by preparing a generation for social efficiency whatever may be the vocation, while laying a foundation for the vocational training which will be received in the graduate schools. Already the growth of graduate departments and graduate schools in this field is remarkable. The leaders of this phase of the movement seem to-day to be wise enough to insist that the standards of this profession shall be as high as that of teachers in public education. In fact, they now urge the student to receive not less than two years of graduate training above the college, and earnestly recommend as teachers of religion that those who aspire to lead shall secure the degree of Doctor of Philosophy. If these leaders have their way, they will see to it that this will not be a profession to be taken up because it requires less of preparation than others. The development of morals and religion in the life of a nation is the hardest of tasks, and only those having the best training should undertake this work as a career.

The Christian home.—After this brief study of the progress of religious education in the Protestant churches of the United States we come back to the one institution of religious instruction upon which all others must rely. The Christian church will make its greatest contribution to the religious progress of the race by developing Christian home-makers. In early times the father was the priest, and most of the religious instruction was imparted by father or mother. During the later centuries some of this responsibility has been shifted from the home to the churches and schools. Some of the responsibility belongs there. These latter agencies must always supplement the home with increasing effectiveness.

But the physical as well as the moral well-being of a race ultimately rests upon the parents. There is no escape from this fact. America has a high ideal of home virtue and home responsibility. At no point has the Christian church of the past in America made so great a contribution to the happiness of its citizens as where it has touched the home. There are perils confronting this institution in these days of so many apartment houses instead of private dwellings, of universal attendance at the moving-picture theaters, and of industrial life which keeps so many women as well as men away from home—perils which never existed before quite so acutely as to-day!

ASSETS AS WELL AS LIABILITIES

However, neither has the world ever had such good schools, churches, playground associations, and other welfare agencies as to-day. If these agencies will intelligently direct their efforts toward improving the family by the preparation and assistance of competent Christian parents, the progress of the race toward the Christian goal is assured. The Sunday school is definitely undertaking this task to-day, and the public school system is giving increasing attention to some phases of it. The colleges are just beginning to see this as a responsibility, and will soon take up the problem more effectively. With a united, intelligent effort on the part of these and other worthy agencies, it seems as if a healthier, nobler race than the world has ever known, a race acknowledging the leadership of Jesus Christ and striving to express his ideals in everyday life, is a probability for the near future.

The problem of leadership.—The movement for religious education, like every other great movement, depends ultimately upon the number and the ability of its leaders. Well might one who has any responsibility for this movement feel humble in the face of so great a task. The nurturing of young lives so that they come from weakness to power is at once the most difficult and most fascinating of tasks. The nurturing of these lives so that they come to strength as the embodiment of the highest type of religion that the world knows is still more difficult. Christianity sets the spiritual goals toward which our race is striving, and for a person to be a living example of this religion he must become as nearly perfect in character as it is possible for a human individual to be.

If Christian educators were striving for a lesser goal, it would be easier to attain; but they deliberately strive for the highest values that they know, and consequently must expect to find their work hard and their labor often disappointing in its results. They know the difficulties, and their own faith in a divine Father's power to help gives them confidence in the ultimate triumph, but they tremble to think how long the victory may be postponed. However, there is no tendency on the part of Christian educators to relax their efforts and to depend upon the Almighty to do their appointed tasks for them. These people are straining every effort to improve materials and technique so that divine love may have better channels through which to operate.

PRESENT TENDENCIES

The movement for the training of teachers and supervisors is depending upon all of the four agencies enumerated, but with especial reliance upon teacher-training in the local churches and in higher institutions of learning. Nearly three quarters of a century have passed since Vincent, Pardee, and others began holding teachers' institutes, and a vast multitude of teachers are still untrained. The public school has been even longer at this task and has achieved more, but still has far to go before adequately meeting its needs. However, it can be said truly that there has never been a time when so many people were in training for these tasks as to-day, nor a time when the quality of training has been so good.

The materials and methods for the training of teachers of religion are in most places somewhat inferior to those for the development of public-school teachers, but they are producing gratifying results and are being improved constantly. The teacher-training textbooks written to meet the requirements of the present Standard Teacher-Training Course mark a great forward step in this form of literature, while the textbooks now in preparation or recently issued for community training classes and college classes by such publishers as The Abingdon Press, The Pilgrim Press, Charles Scribner's Sons, The University of Chicago Press, and others, give evidence that an adequate literature for leadership training will soon be available.

The very recent awakening of interest upon this subject in the colleges, seminaries, and in graduate departments and schools of religion, is one of the most significant evidences of a new day. John H. Vincent expected this awakening to bear fruit plentifully in the late sixties and in the seventies of the preceding century.

Instead, the seed-sowing and cultivation by these agencies is just beginning. But the harvest will be bountiful in a very few years. In fact, the world is already reaping substantial returns from this effort which has so recently started.

Good statesmanship, educational skill, and patient persistence are necessities of the hour for this movement, and the writer believes that the leaders are exhibiting these qualities to so marked a degree that the future is bright with promise.

SUMMARY

We have taken all too brief a glimpse of just a few of the factors in the general movement for religious education. We have confined our study largely to development in the United States, but with no thought of ignoring the debt which the United States owes to other nations of the world for inspiration and assistance in this field.

Debt to England, Canada, and other countries.— Some of the debt to England we acknowledged in the early chapters, but the limitations of time forbade a detailed study of what other nations have contributed to religious education in the United States. The intimate relationship between the workers of Canada and those of our own country have put us greatly in debt to our neighbors. Those who have sat on international committees know well how much the members from Canada have contributed to the technique and materials now used on this side of the border. The Canadian members upon the International Sunday-School Lesson Committee, in the Sunday-School Council of Evangelical Denominations, and elsewhere, have been men of great strength. In the main the developments in recent years have been the result of intimate cooperation, each country profiting greatly by experiments in the other.

Limitations of this study.—Time would fail one if he attempted to follow up all the lines of investigation which bear upon this subject. Instead, we have attempted to describe the most influential currents in the main stream of Protestant educational development. The Roman Catholic, the Lutheran, and other important systems of religious education, have been omitted from this treatment not because they were unimportant or uninteresting but in order to concentrate attention upon what the writer believed to be the most significant movement. The national system of religious education for the United States will be the outcome of this main stream of thought and activity. The system will doubtless be profoundly modified by other school systems, but it will be very largely the outcome of the factors whose growth has been narrated.

The history in brief.—From a crude but unified system of education in which religion had a dominant place to a complex, splendid system of public education with religious instruction practically eliminated has been one phase of our story. From a crude system of religious instruction with materials ungraded and technique undeveloped, to an elaborate system of graded instruction under competent supervision in thousands of churches, but independent of all State control, is another phase of the story. The third phase deals with the approach to each other of the two systems which, at the beginning of the century, were so independent.

Complete separation of management between church

and State schools will always be the aim of the leading Protestant denominations of America, but close co-operation between the two in the present and succeeding generations is the desire to-day of a great number of influential leaders in both systems. Each needs the other. Public education must have a spiritual dynamic, since it must develop motives that draw their power not from physical but from spiritual passions. Hence the public schools must cooperate with church schools. On the other hand, the church schools need the technical skill and the knowledge of how to organize materials which the public-school workers can impart.

Success depends upon three factors.—Three factors will give to the United States an adequate system of education, a system in which religion has its proper place as a dynamic force in the development of socially efficient citizens. One of the three is an aroused public conscience, the second is a trained leadership, and the third is adeqate technique, including materials, methods, and organization.

To be sure, such a statement is but putting the problem in new form rather than a solving of the problem. But it may help us to see where the emphasis in the next few years needs to be placed. The first factor is at present the most undeveloped and the least certain of the three. Human nature, it seems, will never cease to hope for a short-cut to power, although all experience points to the fact that the Creator works through long, slow, orderly processes to achieve His ends. At present, America is in a mood to work for its goals. Short-cuts did not win the World War, and they have not Americanized incoming alien multitudes, nor have they solved any of America's industrial or social problems. If we can keep America in the mood to work slowly but thoroughly, education will come into its own, and the dream of a Christianized society may be realized.

The movement for trained leadership is developing very encouragingly. More ministers are giving attention to the educational aspects of their ministry than ever before. Labor-union leaders are going to college to prepare for their work. Appreciation of the necessity to equip oneself thoroughly for any form of leadership promises to become universal, and the cause of religious education should realize great benefits from the new spirit which is rapidly developing into a strong passion.

The third factor is also being developed rapidly, as we have tried to indicate in the pages of this book.

Unified system, but dual control.—We have spoken as if America could have a unified system of education in which religion and secular subjects would both have their proper place. We believe that this is possible. The system will not be under one management, either of the state or of the church. Both the States and the churches will perfect their own systems, but in cooperation, as we have tried to indicate. The principle of extra-mural credit, so universally accepted in the public-school system, gives an opportunity for each pupil to present credits in religion in every community where the churches and public-school men are progressive and helpful to each other. The system of affiliated colleges and foundations at State universities and the cordial cooperation between State and privately endowed institutions of higher learning has made success here an assured fact.

The will to conquer by love and service.—The French immortalized themselves in the recent World

War by using the phrase, *Ils ne passerant pas*, "They shall not pass," when the greatest physical resources were clearly on the side of the enemy, and only indomitable spiritual resources stood between them and defeat. The will to conquer checked the enemy, when resistance seemed hopeless, and later led to overwhelming victory. The "will to conquer" in the hearts of Christians backed by the wealth of spiritual resources at their command can turn back the forces of ignorance, industrial exploitation, and commercialized vice, which imperil the civilization of this day. In the last analysis, the future of religious education depends upon public opinion. Public opinion is now being aroused. If we develop in Christians the will to conquer by means of love and efficient service, an adequate national system of religious education in the United States will become a fact, and the world will enjoy its benefits.

Questions for discussion:

1. To what extent does the present awakening of interest in religious education seem to you to promise permanency?
2. Analyze the factors which are stimulating this need and the factors which may check its development.
3. Do you believe that the religious instruction of the young is essential to the happiness of this nation and of the world? How would you convince those who disagreed with your answer to this question?
4. What are the principal agencies to be used for the promotion of religious education in the future? Analyze the strong points and weaknesses of each.

5. To what extent will teachers of religion in the local church be paid?

6. What will be the most probable line of development for the week-day church school? Under what auspices will it be conducted in the local community? How should it be promoted nationally?

7. Look up and report on the work of some of the best undergraduate and graduate departments of religious education. Does the nation need great increase in the number of these?

8. What can be done to increase the effectiveness of the home as a teacher of religion?

9. Do the agencies for the promotion of religious education seem to you to be developing an adequate leadership for this movement? What suggestions have you to offer on this subject?

10. How soon do you expect the average boy and girl in the United States to have as fair a chance to learn the fundamental truths about the Bible and religion as they have to learn other important truths?

Brief Bibliography for Special Reference:

Athearn—*A National System of Religious Education.* George H. Doran Company, New York, 1920

Betts—*The New Program of Religious Education.* The Abingdon Press, New York, 1921.

Athearn—*Religious Education and Democracy.* The Pilgrim Press, Boston, 1917.

Stout—*The Organization and Administration of Religion.* Abingdon Press, New York, 1922.

Winchester—*Religious Education in a Democracy.* The Methodist Book Concern, New York, 1917.

Cope—*Education for Democracy*.   University of Chicago Press, Chicago, 1920.

The Church School, current and old files.

Religious Education, current and old files.

Leaflet literature of denominational and other agencies for the promotion of religious education.

INDEX

INDEX

INDEX

INDEX

Kennedy, Mrs. M. G., 106
Kidder, Rev. D. P. (quoted), 69, (quoted), 132f.
Kinley, David, President University of Illinois (quoted), 241
Kinnaird, Rt. Hon. Lord, 172
King's College (Columbia), 229f.
Kinnear, James W., 175
Kirk, Sir John, 172
Knox, George Platt, 188
Knox, John, 24
Krick, Mrs. D. M., 106

Lancaster, Joseph, 53f.
Lancaster System, 53f.
Landes, W. G., 175
Lawrance, Marion, 170, 172ff.
Lawson, Miss Martha K., 107
Legal aspects of week-day church schools, 215f.
Littlefield, Milton S., 106, 159
Louisville International Sunday-School Convention, 110ff.
Loyola, Ignatius, 25
Luther, 24
Lutheran System of religious education, 271

Malden Plan, 157, 245
Mandeville (quoted), 29f.
Mann, Horace, 55, 89
McFarland, John T., 110, 115, 236
McMurray, Charles, 180
McMurray's four tests of a recitation, 17
Methodist Episcopal Church, teacher training of, 155, 160f.
Methodist Episcopal Church, South, teacher training of, 155, 158, 254
Meyer, Henry H., 107
Michigan, University of, 231, 240
Miller, J. R., 110, 115
Miller, Lewis, 78
Miller, Rufus W., 188
Missionary curriculum materials, 114f.
Monastic Schools, 22f.

Moninger's manual of teacher training, 145
Moody Bible Institute, 157
Moody, Dwight L., 140, 171
Moravian Brethren, 26

National Primary Union, 81, 101ff.
National Series of Lessons, 96
National Sunday-School conventions, 70, 168f.
Neighborhood House, Gary, 206
New England Primer, 37ff., 88
New Jersey School of Methods, 102f., 148, 158
Newman, Cardinal, 20
Newton, Richard, 98
New York State Sunday-School Association, 171
New York Sunday-School Union, 50, 166
"Normal College" for Sunday-School teacher training, 140ff.
Normal Schools, 54f., 130f.
"Normal Sunday Schools," 132
North Dakota plan of high-school credit, 201f.
Northwestern Female College, 228f.
Northwestern University, 228f., 235, 245f.
Noyes, Vera L., 206

Oak Park (Illinois) church schools, 213, 246
Oliver, Charles A., 145, 159f.
Origen, 22
Owens, Thomas, 206
Oxford, University of, 24

Paid teachers of religion, 222f., 265
Palestine Class, 77, 139
Pantænus, 20
Pardee, R. G., 70, 77; (quoted), 138, 269
Paris, University of, 23f.
Paxson, Stephen, 55ff., 167, 170
Paxton, Miss Elizabeth, 107
Peabody, Rev. Professor, letter of 1829 (quoted), 61f.

280

INDEX

INDEX

Toronto International Sunday-School Convention, 108
Townley, Colonel, 47
Trumbull, H. Clay, 82ff., 142, 162, 170
Tyler, J. Bennett, 142
Tyng, Alexander G., 98
Tyng, Dr. Stephen H., 54f., (quoted), 63

Uniform Lesson System, developed 95ff.
"Union Questions," 92
Union Theological Seminary, 244
Universities, mediæval, 23f.
University of Chicago Press, 244, 269
Utah plan of religious education for high-school students, 212f.

Van Wert plan of week-day religious instruction, 210f.
Vaughn, H. R., 198, 200
Verse-a-Day system, 92
Vincent, John H., 69f., (quoted), 76f., 78, 82, 95ff., 134ff., (quoted), 136ff., 146, 162, 172, (quoted), 228f., 269

Wanamaker, John, 175
Wardle, Addie Grace, 48
Warren, E. K., 172, 175
Washington, University of, 240
Watts' (Isaac) Cradle Hymn, 39; catechisms, 58f.

Webster's American Spelling Book, 51, 88
Week-day church schools, 185, 195ff., 263f.
Week-day religious instruction, 195ff., 263f.
Weigle, Luther A., 120, 188
Wells, Ralph, 70
Wesley, John, 26, 47, 166
Wesley College, North Dakota, 240
Wesleyan Revival, 45f.
Wesley Foundation, University of Illinois, 241f.
Wesley Foundations, 242f.
Weston, Sidney A., 107, 159
White, Bishop, 49
Whiting (Indiana) church schools, 210
William and Mary College, 229
Wilson, H. E., 206
Winchester, B. S., 107, 110, 115
Wirt, William A., 205ff.
Woodruff, A., 74
World's Sunday-School Association, 72ff., 186
World's Sunday-School Conventions, 172ff.

Yale University, 229
Young Men's Christian Association in colleges, 243
Young Women's Christian Association in colleges, 243

Zwingli, 24
Zinzendorf, 26